# THE ALLERGY-FREE COOK
# Bakes Bread

## GLUTEN-FREE, DAIRY-FREE, EGG-FREE

Laurie Sadowski

BOOK PUBLISHING COMPANY
Summertown Tennessee

*Pictured on the front cover:* Wholesome Flax Bread, 99

*Pictured on the back cover:* Banana-Nut Monkey Bread, 82; Chocolate-Filled Pumpkin Cinnamon Rolls, 86

Cover photos: Warren Jefferson
Cover and interior design: John Wincek

© 2011 Laurie Sadowski
Photos © 2011 Book Publishing Company

Book Publishing Company
P.O. Box 99
Summertown, TN 38483
888-260-8458
www.bookpubco.com

ISBN: 978-1-57067-262-0

Printed in Canada

17 16 15 14 13 12      9 8 7 6 5 4 3 2

Library of Congress Cataloging-in-Publication Data

Sadowski, Laurie.
  The allergy-free cook bakes bread / Laurie Sadowski.
    p. cm.
  Includes index.
    ISBN 978-1-57067-262-0 (pbk.) -- ISBN 978-1-57067-948-3 (e-book)
  1. Gluten-free diet. 2. Gluten-free diet--Recipes. 3. Wheat-free diet--Recipes. 4. Bread. I. Title.
    RM237.86.S23 2011
    641.5'63--dc23
                                  2011032145

Calculations for the nutritional analyses in this book are based on the average number of servings listed with the recipes and the average amount of an ingredient if a range is called for. Calculations are rounded up to the nearest gram. If two options for an ingredient are listed, the first one is used. Not included are fat used for frying (unless the amount is specified in the recipe), optional ingredients, or serving suggestions.

Book Publishing Company is a member of Green Press Initiative. We chose to print this title on paper with 100% post consumer recycled content, processed without chlorine, which saves the following natural resources:

47 trees
1,374 pounds of solid waste
21,681 gallons of water
4,808 pounds of greenhouse gases
19 million BTU of energy

For more information on Green Press Initiative, visit www.greenpressinitiative.org.

Environmental impact estimates were made using the Environmental Defense Fund Paper Calculator. For more information visit www.papercalculator.org.

Printed on recycled paper

BOOK PUBLISHING COMPANY

green press INITIATIVE

# Contents

*Preface* iv
*Acknowledgments* v
*Introduction* vi

## PART I

## Gluten, Food Allergies, and Veganism 1

## PART II

## Gluten-Free Ingredients and Tips for Success 9

## PART III

## Quick Breads 25

SWEET QUICK BREADS 28
SAVORY QUICK BREADS 50

## PART IV

## Yeast Breads 71

SWEET YEAST BREADS 75
SAVORY YEAST BREADS 98

## PART V

## The Extras 121

GLOSSARY 121
SUPPLIERS AND RESOURCES 129
INDEX 131

# Preface

I love baked goods. Chances are, you do too. Who doesn't want a slice of home-style banana bread, dotted with sweet chocolate chips? Or a gooey, sweet cinnamon roll? Or a wholesome loaf of bread, fresh out of the oven?

Unfortunately, for many people, these foods, when conventionally made, have become off limits. Each year, more and more people are diagnosed with celiac disease; an estimated 1 in 133 must adopt a gluten-free diet in order to maintain their health. Furthermore, many people are shifting toward a diet free of animal-based products, including dairy and eggs, as they become more aware of the positive effects such a diet has on their health, the animals, and the environment.

This book supplies guidance and recipes for those who are hungry to learn how to feed their bellies safely, compassionately, nutritiously, and deliciously. For people with celiac disease, it is a primer on eating gluten-free. For families living with autism or ADHD, it delivers information about a casein-free diet. For folks adopting a diet free of animal-based foods, it provides a rundown on veganism. For those with food allergies, it supplies recipes that are free of common allergens, including dairy, eggs, gluten, and wheat. In addition, many of the recipes are also free of legumes, nightshades, nuts, peanuts, seeds, and soy. Finally, this book presents recipes for wholesome, delicious baked goods for anyone who loves to create in the kitchen.

Regardless of why you've picked up this book, I hope it provides you with the reassurance that restricted ingredients *do not* equal restricted diets.

To total wellness and a satisfied stomach,
Laurie Sadowski

# Acknowledgments

This book has been far from a solo effort, regardless of what the cover indicates. First, thank you to Dr. Wayne Gruber, who recognized an illness that wasn't all in my head. Thank you also to Dr. Jane Lauermeier, who has helped me on my journey to wellness, with full respect for my vegan lifestyle.

I am very thankful for the folks at Book Publishing Company, who believed in my concept and put it into being. Specifically, Cynthia Holzapfel, Jo Stepaniak, Beth Geisler, and Barbara Jefferson, who guided me through the steps to get here.

To my wonderful mom and dad, who had to endure the process of eating loads of baked goods—I know how difficult that was for you. And to the rest of my family, especially UM, Grandma and Grandpa, Chrissy, and Mat and X, who were subject to do the same. Extra thanks to UM and Dad, who built the kitchen of my dreams for me.

To Gretchen and the rest of my tasters and testers, your feedback was much appreciated and motivating. Thank you.

To Andrea, Kal, and Brian at the *St. Catharines Standard*, who gave me a food-writing opportunity that lets me spread the message of veganism in the community. To the staff at *Canadian Living* magazine, who gave me the confidence to do what I love to do.

And to everyone I know or have ever come across in life (even if just for a few minutes), thanks for listening to me constantly talk about food.

# Introduction

For many years I never questioned my health. Growing up, I could only assume that everything in my body was functioning properly. Stressful, frequent bowel movements: normal. Constant upset stomach: normal. Excessive fatigue: normal. I thought everyone was subject to the same experiences.

These assumptions allowed me to accept an undiagnosed illness day after day. Throughout my childhood, my exhaustion and discomfort became increasingly prevalent. Then, in my midteens, I suddenly was hit with a terrible bout of mononucleosis. I missed weeks of school and experienced weight loss and debilitating weakness. My glands were so swollen, it became difficult to breathe. Eventually, after making a trip to the hospital and being pumped full of Percocet and steroids, I finally beat the mono. But did I? My family and I were aware that I was never quite the same after that illness, but we just couldn't pinpoint why.

In college, I began to realize that something was dreadfully wrong. The fatigue and gastrointestinal issues persisted, and I was a neurological mess. My legs were so weak, it became hard to walk. I was experiencing extreme night terrors. I was so tired, just the thought of getting out of bed was torture. I was tested for multiple sclerosis twice, had loads of blood tests, and was told that nothing was wrong.

Then the gastrointestinal symptoms went into overdrive. I had extreme bloating and never-ending thirst. I experienced even more weight loss and was frequenting the bathroom more than twenty-five times a day. Something was definitely wrong, and it became shockingly apparent when my weight dropped to seventy-eight pounds. At 5 feet 7½ inches, this extreme thinness wasn't exactly something I could hide.

At last, I was diagnosed with celiac disease in August 2005. The neurological symptoms and most of the gastrointestinal symptoms were alleviated when I adopted a gluten-free diet. However, the stomach pain, bloating, and dizziness lessened only after I stopped consuming casein, a milk protein. Weight flowed back to my body, my energy skyrocketed, and I could live again. Essentially, I was free!

Except, at first, I didn't really feel that way. You see, having been a food writer and critic for my university newspaper, I despaired about all the foods that I was sure would never again pass my lips. So I turned to a resource that offered me much solace in my time of sickness: the Food Network.

The cooking shows inspired me. I spent many hours watching the chefs, learning techniques, and gathering information. I realized, suddenly, that I could still enjoy the same foods, with some modifications. I would not be required to live without my favorites after all.

And so I began—cooking at first, then baking up a storm. With a desire to fulfill my passion for sweet, savory, sour, salty, and spicy, I picked up my spatula and said my final good-byes to gluten. For people who are new to a gluten-free diet, baking tends to be the most difficult skill to remaster. I found myself in an unfamiliar world of gluten-free flour, xanthan gum, sticky batter, and crumbly dough. I was learning and testing and eating and asking my family (the testers) over and over, "Is it good? Is it *really* good or *gluten-free* good?" I demanded answers. I wanted my recipes to taste "just like the real thing."

Eventually I got to yeast breads, which was exciting; I had never baked yeast breads before. Luckily, my bread turned out tasty on the first try. I chalked that up to my inexperience with yeast: I wasn't expecting a punchable loaf. I had read that gluten-free "dough" was supposed to look like batter, and I followed the general guideline of letting the bread rise only once. I was ecstatic, having read about many misadventures in creating gluten-free breads. I posted the recipe on the Internet, and comments starting filing in. They inspired me so much that I decided to write a cookbook.

I self-published *Mission in the Kitchen*, a cookbook dedicated to gluten-free, casein-free, and whole-foods cuisine. I wanted everyone to be able to eat safely, while satisfying his or her needs. Feedback kept pouring in.

Soon I adopted a vegan lifestyle, free of animal products. Along the way, I made it a personal undertaking to prove to others that gluten-free vegan food could taste just as good as "normal" food. I began writing a monthly food column for my local newspaper, spreading the word about gluten-free diets and veganism. I qualified as a top-four finalist in a national cooking competition with a gluten-free vegan dish (I lost to lobster). I wanted to show others that the only restrictions we have are the ones we impose on ourselves.

I'm frequently asked what I eat. In response, I rattle off the basics—fruits, legumes, nuts, and vegetables—and the not-so-basics—nori, quinoa, and teff. When I mention sandwiches or muffins, I'm inevitably met with a surprised look, followed by, "How is it possible to bake without wheat flour, butter, and milk?" I know people will balk if I tell them, "Oh, you know, with sorghum flour, coconut oil, and almond milk." So I just give them a gooey doughnut and, fancy that, they don't say another word . . . until they ask for a second one.

Nourishing our bodies healthfully is the best gift we can give ourselves. Just because we choose to live a vegan lifestyle or we must eat a gluten-free diet doesn't mean we have to lose touch with our taste buds. This book is filled with healthful gluten-free vegan recipes, complete with classic essentials, a few indulgences, and everything in between. Now go make your bread . . . and eat it too.

## PART I

# Gluten, Food Allergies, and Veganism

**W**heat is a mainstay of the modern diet. Chances are, if you are gluten intolerant, you hear this question a lot: "So, what *can* you eat?" This common inquiry is often followed by this astonished realization: "Wait a second. You can't eat *bread*?" Hold the phone: I'm here to tell you that *of course* you can eat bread! This book was written to show you how to make many delicious, gluten-free varieties.

So what is this "gluten," anyway? Gluten is a protein found in wheat, rye, and barley that helps bind baked goods and hold in moisture. The term literally is translated from the Latin word *gluten*, meaning "glue." Gluten-containing flours, such as wheat flour, give elasticity and cohesiveness to dough, help dough rise, and give the finished product a chewy texture.

For many people, eating gluten isn't a problem. For others, including those with celiac disease (like me), gluten triggers debilitating symptoms, such as abdominal pain, bloating, chronic diarrhea (or constipation), cramping, fatigue, and weight loss (and sometimes, in adults, weight gain). Celiac disease is an autoimmune disorder that interferes with the small intestine's ability to absorb nutrients and can be difficult to diagnose.

Adopting a lifelong gluten-free diet is the only way to heal the gut and treat celiac disease. At first I found this news devastating. Then I discovered

> *The doctor of the future will no longer treat the human frame with drugs, but rather will cure and prevent disease with nutrition.*
>
> **—THOMAS EDISON**

that, with a little know-how, I can enjoy a wide variety of nourishing, satisfying, tasty—and, yes, even decadent—foods, including my favorite: baked goods.

However, those who are new to gluten-free baking may find themselves in a bit of a conundrum. How is it possible to mimic gluten's magic? The answer is simpler than you might think: Although you are no longer reliant on wheat flour, you can choose from more than twenty varieties of gluten-free flours that are delicious and often nutritionally superior. In place of wheat flour, my recipes call for wholesome flours made from amaranth, buckwheat, chickpeas, millet, quinoa, sorghum, teff, and more. Don't worry if you've never heard of some of these. I provide plenty of information about gluten-free flours in part II (page 9). These products are increasingly available in supermarkets. If you are unable to find them there, many online retailers sell gluten-free baking supplies (see Suppliers and Resources, page 129). Ironically, adopting a gluten-free diet may be just the thing to help you realize how *many* choices you really have.

People who are gluten intolerant may also be lactose intolerant. That's why my recipes are free of dairy products. In fact, I am a vegan and use no animal-based foods at all in my baking. Another reason that I eliminated dairy products from my baked goods is that people with celiac disease may be allergic or sensitive to casein (a milk protein). I also am aware that it is not uncommon for those with celiac disease or food allergies to have other food sensitivities. In consideration of this fact, for each recipe I clearly indicate which common allergens are absent.

## CHECK ALLERGEN INFORMATION FOR EACH RECIPE

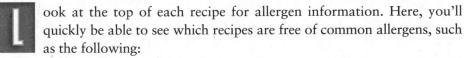ook at the top of each recipe for allergen information. Here, you'll quickly be able to see which recipes are free of common allergens, such as the following:

**Legumes.** Recipes that are free of legumes do not include beans, such as chickpeas or chickpea flour. They are also free of peanuts (which are actually a legume, not a nut), soybeans, and soy products and derivatives.

**Nightshades.** Recipes that are free of nightshades do not include ingredients such as cayenne, paprika, peppers, potato, potato starch, and tomato. If a recipe calls for potato starch, substitute an equal amount of arrowroot starch, cornstarch, or tapioca flour. Note: Sweet potato and black pepper are *not* nightshades.

**Nuts.** Recipes that are free of nuts do not include tree nuts, such as almonds, hazelnuts, pecans, and walnuts. For any recipe that contains nuts, the nuts can typically be omitted without affecting the taste. Note: Recipes that are free of tree nuts may include coconut, peanuts, or seeds.

**Peanuts.** Recipes that are free of peanuts do not include peanut butter. Because peanuts are legumes, any recipes that contain peanuts will also contain legumes. Note: Recipes that are peanut-free may include nuts or seeds.

**Seeds.** Recipes that are free of seeds do not include caraway, chia, flax, hemp, sesame, or other seeds. Note: Recipes that are seed-free may include nuts.

**Soy.** Recipes that are free of soy do not include any form of soy, such as tofu. Note: If you are unable to consume soy, be sure to use a soy-free vegan buttery spread. Many buttery spreads contain some soy, so recipes in this book that include vegan buttery spread are not listed as legume- or soy-free. However, these recipes can be made soy-free by using soy-free vegan buttery spread or substituting with oil.

## READ FOOD LABELS CAREFULLY

B ecause an increasing number of people are sensitive to gluten, food labels are now more likely to indicate whether an item contains gluten. Despite increasingly strict labeling laws, gluten still slips into products. Although you might not expect to find it there, gluten can be in all types of processed foods, including bouillon, broth, condiments, dressings, energy bars, miso paste, rice cheese and soy cheese, and soy sauce. In addition, gluten shows up in even more unexpected places, such as cosmetics and shampoos. Bear in mind that gluten might find its way into your mouth via toothpaste or even pet food, if your pet delivers sloppy kisses. It can even turn up in church: communion wafers contain gluten.

One strategy for avoiding gluten is to cut down on processed foods. Instead, pack your diet with whole foods, including fresh fruits and vegetables, nutritious gluten-free grains, fiber-rich legumes, nutrient-dense nuts and seeds, and plain organic tempeh and tofu. When a food contains a single ingredient—the food itself—there is no room for confusion. This style of eating is not only a safe way to approach a gluten-free vegan diet, but it is also exceedingly healthful.

When you do buy packaged foods, vigilance is required. Table 1 (page 4) provides some guidelines on how to interpret food labels to identify "hidden" sources of gluten or dairy. If you are ever confused or suspicious, don't hesitate to call the food manufacturer. Most companies are more than pleased to provide information.

| TABLE 1 | Common terms for items and ingredients containing gluten, dairy, or egg products |
|---|---|
| **INGREDIENT** | **WORDS TO LOOK FOR** |
| Wheat | Bran, bread flour, brown flour, bulgur, durum, enriched flour, farina, faro, germ, gluten, graham, groats, hydrolyzed wheat protein, Kamut (khorasan wheat), roux, seitan, semolina, spelt, triticum, udon (wheat noodles), wheat starch |
| Barley | Barley grass, barley groats, barley malt, barley syrup, beer, brown rice syrup (could contain barley), malt, pearl barley |
| Dairy/casein | All dairy products, artificial butter flavor, butter, butter oil, butterfat, buttermilk, casein, caseinates (ammonia, calcium, magnesium, potassium, sodium), cheese, cottage cheese, cream, curds, custard, ghee, goat's milk, half-and-half, hydrolysates (casein, milk protein, whey), ice milk, kefir, lactalbumin phosphate, lactate, lactic acid, lactoglobulin, lactose, lactulose, margarine, milk (condensed, dry, evaporated, malted, powdered, skim, whole), milk fat, milk protein, milk solids, nougat, pudding, rennet, sherbet, spread, whey, yogurt |
| Eggs | Albumin, binder, coagulant, eggs (powdered, white, whole, yolk, or yellow), emulsifier, lecithin, livetin, lysozyme, ovalbumin, ovamucin, ovamucoid, ovovitellin, vitellin |
| Other (check with the manufacturer) | Artificial flavors, avena (oats), bread, breading, cereal, chocolate, couscous, croutons, hydrolyzed vegetable or soy protein, imitation bacon, oatmeal, oats, rye, starch |

## AVOID CROSS-CONTAMINATION

Beyond checking labels, it's important to be aware of the possibility that foods may be cross-contaminated with gluten. Cross-contamination can occur when gluten-free grains and gluten-containing grains are processed in the same mill or cereal plant. For example, people who are gluten intolerant are advised to avoid oats because the likelihood of contamination is significant. The good news is that some companies take a great deal of care to avoid cross-contamination; however, many do not. People with gluten intolerance and food allergies are wise to become familiar with companies whose practices they can trust. Nevertheless, keep in mind that companies change their formulations from time to time, so it's wise to check the labels of even those products you purchase regularly.

Cross-contamination may also happen in homes and restaurants. Food may be contaminated by equipment that has been used to prepare foods containing gluten. For example, cross-contamination may occur if crumbs are left in a toaster, pasta residue remains in a colander, or utensils are shared between dishes. If you live in a household that stocks foods that contain gluten, here are some helpful tips.

**Designate a "gluten-free zone" in the kitchen or pantry.** Set aside an area exclusively for gluten-free goods and ingredients. Or, if these foods make up the bulk of your household's provisions, have an area for "unsafe" foods. Keep crumbly cereals in a designated section of the pantry. Store gluten-containing and gluten-free baking ingredients in sealed containers in separate cabinets.

**Specify kitchen items for gluten-free use only.** Reserve one set of small appliances, such as a blender, bread maker, can opener, mixer, and toaster, for use only with gluten-free foods and ingredients. Crumbs and other miniscule food remnants can lurk in this equipment.

Certain items, such as cast-iron pans, cookware with nonstick coating, cutting boards, and wooden spoons can be porous and harbor contaminants. Having extra of each is a good idea.

Starchy foods, such as pasta, can leave residue inside colanders. Have a colander specifically for gluten-free use. Alternatively, serve only gluten-free pastas. There are some brands of pasta that taste similar to wheat pasta—Tinkyada, made from brown rice, is one. Your family may even prefer the gluten-free alternative.

**Carefully manage open condiments and staples.** Cross-contamination can occur when a spoon or other utensil is inserted into more than one condiment jar. Buy two sets of condiments or other common staples. Clearly mark one set for use only by the gluten-sensitive members of your household.

Ditch any old baking powder, baking soda, and other baking essentials that may remain from your gluten days. Chances are you used the same measuring spoon to dip into these ingredients along with the wheat flour.

**Take precautions during and after shopping.** Say good-bye to the bulk section of the grocery store. Most folks don't think twice about using the scoop for the oats inside the scoop for the cornstarch.

Be sure to wash produce well when you come home from the store. Bags of wheat flour can leave a residue on the conveyor at checkout, and it can easily contaminate fruits and vegetables.

**Be prepared.** If you opt to eat out at restaurants or other peoples' homes, do so with the utmost care. Is the convenience worth it? If so, take all the necessary precautions.

Always carry snacks with you. Being famished is a terrible feeling. A baggie of trail mix, a homemade muffin, a piece of fruit, or sliced veggies can at least tide you over until you can enjoy a full meal. Whenever I leave for the day, I carry a cooler packed with lunch and snacks—just in case.

I hope these tips help you get started on the path to living gluten-free safely. As you become more comfortable with your new lifestyle, you'll find that most of these precautions become second nature.

## VEGANISM 101

Vegans, unlike vegetarians, avoid using all animal-based products. Dairy, eggs, gelatin, and honey are bid *adieu*, often alongside leather, wool, and items from companies that test on animals. Just as you might have been surprised to learn that many foods unexpectedly contain gluten, you might also be surprised to find animal-based products in certain consumer goods. For example, wine can be clarified with albumin (from eggs), casein (a milk protein), gelatin (from bones), and isinglass (from fish). In addition, some foods contain added vitamin $D_3$, which is animal derived. (Note that $D_2$ is the vegan form of this vitamin.)

There are many reasons to adopt a vegan diet. For many people, the primary concern is animal suffering, given that the vast majority of animal-based foods now come from factory farms, where animals are subjected to unnatural confinement, overcrowding, debeaking, tail docking, and other atrocities.

Folks who are concerned about the environment may also embrace a vegan lifestyle. In 2010, the United Nations Environment Programme reported that the global population will reach 9.1 billion people by 2050, and the consumption of animal products will be unsustainable. Today, animal agriculture is the greatest consumer of some of the world's natural resources. Meat and dairy products, in particular, account for 70 percent of freshwater consumption and 38 percent of total land use. In addition, animal agriculture is responsible for 19 percent of total greenhouse gas emissions.

Others are attracted to veganism for the health benefits. The consumption of meat, dairy, and eggs has been linked to many ailments, including cancer and heart disease. In 2009, the American Dietetic Association published a report stating that vegetarian diets are associated with many health benefits, such as lower blood cholesterol and reduced risk of cancer, cardiovascular disease, and type 2 diabetes. The report also states that vegetarians tend to have a lower body mass index (BMI) and, overall, have diets that are richer in fiber and nutrients. Vegetarian and vegan diets have also been positively associated with alleviating symptoms of Crohn's disease and mitigating childhood obesity. The combination of a gluten-free *and* vegan diet has been shown to benefit rheumatoid arthritis.

It's up to the individual to determine how far to go with the vegan life-style, and which foods and products to avoid. Some people with celiac disease, for example, may suffer from severe malabsorption and may decide not to adopt a vegan diet. I encourage working with your doctor and naturopath to find the best solution for you.

If you are already a gluten-free vegan or in the transitional process of adopting this dual lifestyle, it's important to ensure that your restrictions aren't barring you from optimal health. It is essential that a gluten-free vegan diet, like any other, is balanced, nutritious, and abundant in satisfying, wholesome foods. Living on gluten-free pasta, apple juice, and peanut butter isn't ideal for anyone, regardless of dietary restrictions. Keep tabs on what you're eating, making sure your diet is well rounded and rich in all vitamins and nutrients.

If you're not a vegan, keep in mind that you, too, can make veganism a part of your life. Enjoying a vegan dinner, even just once per week, is a great way to start and will benefit your health, the environment, and animal welfare.

## Watch for Gluten in Meat Analogs

Vegans may be familiar with gluten as a food product, also known as seitan or "wheat meat." Gluten is also a popular ingredient in many veggie burgers, meatless hot dogs, and many other meat alternatives. Be wary of these foods if veganism is new to you.

## PART II

# Gluten-Free Ingredients and Tips for Success

By now, you've made a conscious decision to dive into the world of gluten-free and vegan baking. With so many ingredient substitutions, you may feel a little overwhelmed. That's okay—I'll break it down for you.

## XANTHAN GUM

If you haven't done any gluten-free baking, xanthan gum may be new to you. The name is hardly catchy. However, gluten-free cooks know that xanthan gum is magical. It imparts a gluten-like consistency, but without the gluten. It also acts as a binding agent, holding all the other ingredients together. Note that xanthan gum is made from corn. If you must avoid corn, use guar gum, which is made from legumes, instead. An equal amount of guar gum can be substituted for xanthan gum.

At first, using xanthan gum can be a process of trial and error. Over time, however, you'll get the hang of using this newfound staple. Table 2 (page 10) lists how much xanthan gum to use in different types of recipes.

*Everything should be made as simple as possible, but not simpler.*

—ALBERT EINSTEIN

| TABLE 2 | Recommended amounts of xanthan gum |
|---|---|
| **FOOD** | **AMOUNT OF XANTHAN GUM (OR GUAR GUM)** |
| Bread and pizza crust | 1 teaspoon per 1 cup of gluten-free flour |
| Cakes, muffins, and quick breads | ½ teaspoon per 1 cup of gluten-free flour |
| Cookies and bars | ¼ teaspoon per ½ cup of gluten-free flour |

## GLUTEN-FREE FLOURS AND STARCHES

Remember the old days, when baking with all-purpose flour meant that one type of flour did the job? Gluten-free baking is different. Standard practice is to combine two or more types of flour in each recipe. Single flours don't work well on their own, and flour combinations are typically married with a gluten-free starch.

You can buy premixed combinations of gluten-free flour by the bag, but where's the fun in that? I recommend mixing your own, like I do. For example, I often pair quinoa flour and teff flour for their high protein content, distinctive flavors, and nutrient-rich profiles. To balance this, I add a starch, such as arrowroot, to deliver a lighter finished product. To round out the mix, I like the neutral taste and nutritional qualities of sorghum flour. The end result is similar to wheat-based baked goods.

Each gluten-free flour has a unique taste and texture. Different flours also have different nutritional values and perform certain tasks better than others. Coming up with your own mixture of gluten-free flours doesn't have to be difficult. The key is knowing the properties of each type of flour, and this becomes easier with practice. Here's what you need to know about the many gluten-free flours and starches.

**Amaranth flour.** Amaranth flour has a nutty and peppery taste and is a little on the sweet side. I love its toasted flavor in bread and in gravy, where I use it as a thickener. It is high in protein and rich in calcium and fiber. When baking, use it for up to 25 percent of the total flour in your flour mix. To convert conventional recipes to gluten-free versions, replace each cup of all-purpose flour with 1 scant cup of amaranth flour.

**Arrowroot starch.** Arrowroot starch is also known as arrowroot flour and adds body and texture when paired with heavier gluten-free flours. It works well as a thickener and, unlike cornstarch, does not become chalky if under-cooked. It is a good alternative to cornstarch if you are corn-free. Arrowroot starch can be substituted with potato starch or tapioca flour. I prefer this starch to others because it has a little extra fiber. As a thickener, it should be made into a slurry before being added to hot liquid. To convert conventional recipes to gluten-free versions, replace each cup of all-purpose flour with 1 scant cup of arrowroot starch.

**Buckwheat flour.** Compared to other flours, buckwheat flour is an excellent source of high-quality protein, and it is also rich in fiber and zinc. Its distinct flavor makes it a good choice for breads, muffins, and pancakes. To convert conventional recipes to gluten-free versions, replace each cup of all-purpose flour with 1 cup of buckwheat flour, less 1 tablespoon.

**Chestnut flour.** Chestnut flour adds sweetness and moisture to baked goods. For these tasks, it performs comparably to bean flours. Popular in Italy and France, chestnut flour is becoming more common in North America.

**Chickpea flour.** Chickpea flour is high in fiber and protein and adds moisture and texture to baked goods. Some people do not like its strong taste. When baking, use it for up to 25 percent of the total flour in your flour mix. To convert conventional recipes to gluten-free versions, replace each cup of all-purpose flour with ¾ cup of chickpea flour.

**Coconut flour.** Coconut flour is higher in fiber and fat and lower in carbohydrates than most gluten-free flours. Up to 20 percent of the total amount of flour called for in a given recipe can be coconut flour. Coconut flour has an extremely high fiber content that readily absorbs wet ingredients, so be sure to proportionately increase the amount of liquid if using coconut flour to convert a conventional recipe.

**Corn flour.** Corn flour, or masa harina, is made from dried corn that has been slaked (soaked in lime water), dehulled, and ground. It is most often used for tortillas and tamales but also makes a nice addition to pastry crusts. To convert conventional recipes to gluten-free versions, replace each cup of all-purpose flour with 1 cup of corn flour.

**Cornmeal.** Cornmeal is coarser than corn flour and available in white, yellow, and blue. I have trouble finding the white and blue varieties where I live, so the recipes in this book all use the yellow variety. Often the featured ingredient in cornbread and polenta, cornmeal provides a dense, crumbly texture. It also makes a tasty coating for tofu. To convert conventional recipes to gluten-free versions, replace each cup of all-purpose flour with ¾ cup of cornmeal.

**Cornstarch.** Cornstarch is the powdery substance inside of the corn kernel. Tasteless and fine, it is most often used as a thickening agent or in combination with other flours. If you are corn-free, you can replace cornstarch measure for measure with arrowroot starch, potato starch, or tapioca flour. As a thickener, cornstarch should be made into a slurry before being added to hot liquid. To convert conventional recipes to gluten-free versions, replace each cup of all-purpose flour with ¾ cup of cornstarch.

**Garfava flour.** Garfava flour is a combination of chickpea (or garbanzo bean) flour and fava bean flour, and has a less distinct taste than either of these flours alone. To convert conventional recipes to gluten-free versions, replace each cup of all-purpose flour with 1 scant cup of garfava flour.

**Millet flour.** Millet flour is a little sweet and delivers a good crumb in baked goods. It is nutritious and rich in B vitamins. To convert conventional recipes to gluten-free versions, replace each cup of all-purpose flour with 1 cup of millet flour.

**Nut flours.** Also known as nut meals, nut flours are high in fiber and fat. They add moisture, flavor, and texture to baked goods. Almond flour is the most common, but hazelnut and pecan flours can also be found pretty easily. To convert conventional recipes to gluten-free versions, replace each cup of all-purpose flour with 1 cup of nut flour. Note: If you have a recipe that calls for powdered milk, almond flour makes a great replacement.

**Oats.** There are now companies that produce certified gluten-free oats, the only type of oats deemed safe for people with celiac disease. People who are gluten intolerant should check with their health-care providers before including these oats in their diets.

**Potato flour.** Potato flour, not to be confused with potato *starch*, is ground from whole potatoes and is heavy and dense. It works well as a thickener and should only be used in very small amounts. It is sometimes used in commercial flour mixes. To convert conventional recipes to gluten-free versions, replace each cup of all-purpose flour with ½ cup of potato flour.

**Potato starch.** Potato starch is also often called potato starch flour, but it shouldn't be confused with potato *flour*. It is very fine and, like other starches, works well as a thickener and should be made into a slurry before being added to hot liquid. It bakes well at high temperatures and adds moistness to baked goods. To convert conventional recipes to gluten-free versions, replace each cup of all-purpose flour with ¾ cup of potato starch.

**Quinoa flour.** Quinoa is a personal favorite, and I use it to add protein and nutrients to gluten-free recipes. It has a very distinct flavor. If you don't like the strong taste of quinoa flour, replace one-half of the quinoa flour with amaranth, bean, or millet flour. To convert conventional recipes to gluten-free versions, replace each cup of all-purpose flour with 1 cup of quinoa flour.

**Rice flour.** There are three main types of rice flour: white, sweet, and brown. White rice flour is a common replacement for wheat flours in many commercial products and gluten-free recipes; it is also a primary component of most gluten-free flour mixes.

Sweet rice flour is also called "glutinous rice flour" or just "glutinous flour." Don't be alarmed by this terminology. Rice flours contain no gluten; rather, the term refers to the sticky texture of the rice. Sweet rice flour adds lightness and texture to baked goods. Like the various starches, it works well as a thickener for gravies and sauces.

Brown rice flour is nutty and coarse but packs more nutrition than its white counterparts. To convert conventional recipes to gluten-free versions, replace each cup of all-purpose flour with 1 cup of rice flour, less 1 tablespoon.

**Sorghum flour.** Sorghum flour has a high protein content and is smoother than most other flours. It is a component in many flour mixes, has a slight molasses flavor, and is rich in nutrients. Most of my recipes use sorghum flour. I like it for its taste and texture, and I appreciate its lower cost. To convert conventional recipes to gluten-free versions, replace each cup of all-purpose flour with 1 scant cup of sorghum flour.

**Soy flour.** Just like soybeans, soy flour is high in protein and fat, with a strong flavor. Most soy flours are defatted. Similar to other bean flours, soy flour adds moisture and texture to baked goods. To convert conventional recipes to gluten-free versions, replace each cup of all-purpose flour with 1 scant cup of soy flour.

**Tapioca flour.** Also known as tapioca starch, this flour is made from the cassava plant and is suitable for baking and thickening. It delivers a moist texture in baked goods, giving it the "chew factor" that people often look for. As a thickener, it should be made into a slurry before being added to hot liquid. To convert conventional recipes to gluten-free versions, replace each cup of all-purpose flour with 1 cup of tapioca flour.

**Teff flour.** High in protein, slightly sweet, and somewhat nutty, teff flour is another one of my favorites. It is the main ingredient in a fermented Ethiopian bread called *injera* and works well in savory breads and darker, denser cakes and cookies, such as gingerbread. To convert conventional recipes to gluten-free versions, replace each cup of all-purpose flour with 1 cup of teff flour, less 1 tablespoon.

You may want to substitute my choice of flours for many reasons: to correspond with your own tastes, to use a more healthful option, or to use what is readily available. For example, some folks swear by rice flour, whereas I find it lacks nutrition, texture, and taste. While many bakers like to use coconut flour, I don't use it much because I never see it in the stores in my area. Furthermore, you may want to swap ingredients to accommodate your intolerances or allergies. Regardless of your reason for making changes, rest assured: these recipes are very forgiving, so feel free to use what works for you.

To substitute one flour for another, choose a flour with a similar protein content for the best results. Amaranth flour and buckwheat flour, for example, interchange well because their protein content is similar and they weigh the same per cup. Each gluten-free flour has a different weight, so it's not always possible to substitute measure for measure. See table 3 (page 15) for details.

## Tweak Tastes with a Little Creativity

Some flours, such as chickpea and quinoa flours, have strong tastes that may not appeal to you. However, that does not mean you have to scratch them from your baking repertoire. Here's the secret: Mask strong-tasting flours with extracts, herbs, and spices.

## CUSTOMIZE RECIPES TO MEET YOUR NEEDS

Once you've said good-bye to gluten and adios to animal products, the following tips may be helpful if you want to adapt some of your favorite old recipes. They may also be useful if you want to adjust the recipes in this book to include less fat or sugar.

**Decrease fat.** Keep a little bit of fat in the recipe or baked goods will have a gummy or chewy texture. I recommend using at least 2 tablespoons of fat. For muffins and quick breads, in place of some of the oil or buttery spread, try using pureed fruit, such as applesauce, bananas, prunes, or pumpkin. Choose a fruit that will enhance the flavor of the recipe.

| TABLE 3 | Nutritional content and weight of gluten-free flours | | | | |
|---|---|---|---|---|---|
| Flour (¼ cup) | Calories, kcal | Fat, grams | Fiber, grams | Protein, grams | Weight, grams |
| Almond flour | 160 | 14 | 3 | 6 | 28 |
| Amaranth flour | 110 | 2 | 3 | 4 | 30 |
| Arrowroot starch | 110 | 0 | 1 | 0 | 32 |
| Buckwheat flour | 100 | 0 | 4 | 4 | 30 |
| Chestnut flour | 90 | 1 | 0 | 1 | 25 |
| Chickpea flour | 110 | 2 | 5 | 6 | 30 |
| Coconut flour | 120 | 3 | 12 | 4 | 28 |
| Corn flour | 110 | 1 | 4 | 2 | 28 |
| Cornmeal | 110 | 1 | 5 | 2 | 32 |
| Cornstarch | 120 | 0 | 0 | 0 | 32 |
| Fava bean flour | 110 | 0.5 | 8 | 9 | 33 |
| Garfava flour | 150 | 2.5 | 3 | 9 | 30 |
| Hazelnut flour | 180 | 17 | 3 | 4 | 28 |
| Millet flour | 110 | 1 | 4 | 3 | 30 |
| Potato flour | 160 | 0.8 | 2.8 | 4 | 45 |
| Potato starch | 160 | 0 | 0 | 0 | 48 |
| Quinoa flour | 120 | 2 | 4 | 4 | 28 |
| Rice flour, brown | 140 | 1 | 1 | 3 | 39.5 |
| Rice flour, sweet white | 180 | 0.5 | 1 | 3 | 51 |
| Rice flours, white | 150 | 0.5 | 1 | 2 | 39.5 |
| Sorghum flour | 120 | 1 | 3 | 4 | 31.75 |
| Soy flour | 120 | 6 | 3 | 10 | 28 |
| Tapioca flour | 100 | 0 | 0 | 0 | 30 |
| Teff flour | 113 | 1 | 4 | 4 | 30 |

Instead of regular coconut milk or tofu, use a lite variety. It does the same job but without the extra fat.

If the recipe calls for nuts or seeds, decrease the amount needed by 25 percent and toast them (see page 20 for instructions). Toasting amplifies the flavor, which helps compensate for the reduced fat.

**Cut calories.** Try unsweetened almond or hempseed milk. These varieties tend to have significantly fewer calories than their sweetened counterparts or soy and rice milks.

**Scale down the sweetener.** Eliminate up to one-third the amount of sugar or other sweetener called for in the recipe. Cutting back on the sugar often doesn't have much effect on how sweet the final product tastes.

Recipes with fruit may need less sugar if the fruit is at peak ripeness. Bake with fruits that are at their seasonal prime.

A food's glycemic index is the measure of the rate at which it causes blood glucose levels to rise. The glycemic index might be of concern to people with diabetes, for example. Agave nectar has a lower glycemic index than refined sugar, and therefore is absorbed more slowly in the bloodstream. See page 22 for substitution instructions.

**Pump up the flavor.** Always use fresh herbs and spices when baking. For example, brand-new cinnamon has much more zing than cinnamon that has been in the pantry for two years.

## SUBSTITUTION CENTRAL: MAKE YOUR BAKED GOODS VEGAN

Once you've said good-bye to gluten, it's time to think vegan. Gluten-free vegan recipes do not include dairy products, eggs, gelatin, honey, or other animal-derived ingredients. Not to worry. There are plenty of alternatives to choose from.

### Instead of Milk

There are many nondairy milk varieties. The trick is knowing which ones work well for different types of baked goods. Each has its own properties, flavor, and ideal uses.

**Coconut milk.** A little thicker than other nondairy milks, coconut milk works well in baking. The lite varieties are a very creamy and tasty alternative to the full-fat versions (and no one will ever miss the fat). Coconut milk produces a moist, flavorful texture and can be substituted for heavy cream in biscuits, custards, puddings, and scones. There are also newer versions of coconut milk, designed for drinking (as opposed to cooking and baking), that are even lower in fat and work similarly to almond milk.

**Nut and seed milks.** Because of their naturally sweet and nutty flavor, nut and seed milks are ideal for desserts. Almond milk, hazelnut milk, and hempseed milk are among my favorites.

**Potato milk.** Although less common than other nondairy options, potato milk tends to whiten baked goods instead of promote browning.

**Rice milk.** Naturally sweet, rice milk is a good choice for baking, although it has a much thinner texture than most other nondairy milks.

**Soymilk.** Available in many flavors, soymilk works well in baking. Note, however, that baked goods made with soymilk have a tendency to brown more quickly than those made with other nondairy milks.

## Vegan Buttermilk

I often refer to "vegan buttermilk" in my recipes when I want to provide a nondairy alternative to this classic baking ingredient. Dairy-based buttermilk is milk that has been cultured, increasing the milk's acidity and causing it to clump together and thicken. To make vegan buttermilk, put 1 tablespoon of lemon juice or cider vinegar in a liquid measuring cup. Pour in as much unsweetened nondairy milk as you need to equal the total amount of buttermilk called for in the recipe. Stir and let stand for 10 minutes. Use nut milk, seed milk, or soymilk for the best results.

## Instead of Butter

Like milk, butter is easily substituted in vegan baking. A vegan buttery spread or a variety of oils will do the trick.

**Vegan buttery spread.** Buttery-tasting vegan spread is sold in tubs or sticks and can be substituted measure for measure for butter in any recipe. I recommend the Earth Balance brand. When shopping for vegan buttery spread, opt for one that is nonhydrogenated and free of trans fats. Also be sure to check labels to avoid hidden dairy products (see page 4) and soy.

**Canola and olive oils.** Canola and olive oils are economical oils that work great when a buttery taste isn't necessary. If you are substituting oil for a solid fat, such as butter or vegan buttery spread, use three parts oil to four parts fat. For example, if a recipe calls for 1 cup of butter, try ¾ cup of oil.

**Coconut oil.** Another popular choice, coconut oil is a nonhydrogenated source of healthful saturated fats. There are two kinds of coconut oil: unrefined and refined. Unrefined has the distinct scent of coconut and costs about twice as much as the refined version. I prefer unrefined coconut oil because it is not heated, bleached, or deodorized; these common practices remove valuable nutrients.

At room temperature (unless your house is very warm), coconut oil will be the texture of softened butter, perfect for beating into a batter. It is liquid when warmed and rock solid when stored in the refrigerator.

## Instead of Eggs

There are a variety of ways to replace eggs in recipes, but not all alternatives offer the same outcome. Select an egg substitute based on the egg's task in a given recipe. For example, if eggs are needed for binding, use ground flaxseeds. If they are added for moisture, opt for pureed fruit. For a creamy texture, try silken tofu, which is a fantastic egg substitute in custards and quiches. I recommend starting with recipes that require only one or two eggs. Table 4 (page 19) provides all the details you need. Note that in conventional recipes, two egg whites are equivalent to one egg.

## TIPS AND TECHNIQUES

Say good-bye to punching down yeast dough and sampling batters. Those days are over. Whether you're using the recipes in this book or adapting your own favorites, here are some techniques that will be critical to your success.

**Make sure ingredients are at the right temperature.** When baking yeast breads, use ingredients that are at room temperature before proceeding. This may require some advance planning, because flours should always be stored in sealed containers in the refrigerator or freezer to avoid rancidity. Conversely, use cold fats and liquids to make biscuits and scones (see page 27).

**Combine dry ingredients thoroughly before adding wet ingredients.** Always use a dry whisk to combine dry ingredients, such as flour, leavener, starch,

| TABLE 4 | Common egg substitutes and their uses | | |
|---|---|---|---|
| **SUBSTITUTE FOR 1 EGG** | **BEST USED IN** | **PURPOSE** | **NOTES** |
| 3 tablespoons warm water whisked with 1 tablespoon ground flaxseeds; let stand until thickened | Breads, cakes, most cookies, muffins, scones | Binder | • Adds fiber and good fats<br>• Adds a bit of a nutty taste<br>• Use golden flaxseeds to avoid brown specks in light-colored baked goods |
| 3 tablespoons water whisked with 1 tablespoon ground chia seeds; let stand until thickened | Breads and muffins | Binder | • Adds fiber and good fats<br>• Does not perform as consistently as ground flaxseeds<br>• Can add a bit of a gummy texture |
| 1½ teaspoons commercial egg replacer mixed with 2 tablespoons warm water | Some cookies, hard icings | Leavener | • Its neutral taste makes it an excellent choice for delicate cookies<br>• Best for cookies with few ingredients, in which ground flaxseeds would be apparent and unattractive |
| ¼ cup pureed silken tofu | Brownies, heavy loaves, pound cake | Binder, moisturizer | • Adds moisture and density |
| ¼ cup mashed or pureed fruit (such as applesauce, bananas, or pumpkin) plus ¼ teaspoon baking powder | Breads, cakes, cupcakes, muffins | Moisturizer | • Adds moisture and density |

and xanthan gum, before combining them with wet ingredients. This step will ensure that the mixture is aerated and the ingredients are evenly distributed.

**Use parchment paper.** Because gluten-free dough can be sticky, line the baking sheet with parchment paper. In addition, when rolling out dough, sandwich it between two sheets of parchment paper, lightly oiling and sprinkling the bottom sheet of parchment paper with arrowroot starch to further discourage sticking.

**Keep an eye on goodies when they are in the oven.** Gluten-free baked goods, especially those made with agave nectar or soymilk, tend to brown more quickly than other baked goods. If you find that baked goods are browning too quickly, use aluminum foil to tent the pan and continue to bake until the items are cooked through. The higher the protein and fat content in the flour, the more quickly the item will tend to brown.

**Test for doneness.**  To test breads and cakes for doneness, insert a toothpick in the center. If the toothpick comes out clean, the item is done. If there is batter on the toothpick, additional baking is required.

Besides using the toothpick test, you can tell by looking at quick breads and muffins whether they are finished baking. These items should be golden in color, and the edges should pull away from the sides of the pan.

To test yeast breads for doneness, insert an instant-read thermometer in the center of the loaf. When the loaf is done, the thermometer will read 200 degrees F. In addition, the crust will be golden, and the bread will sound hollow if you lightly tap it. For more yeast bread baking tips, see page 71.

**Toast nuts and seeds.**  To toast nuts and seeds, spread them on a baking pan in a single layer. Bake at 400 degrees F for about 7 minutes until golden, shaking the pan a few times while baking. To toast nuts and seeds in a skillet, spread them in a single layer. Cook over medium-high heat, stirring often, for 5 to 7 minutes. Toasted nuts and seeds should be fragrant and golden. They burn quickly, so be sure to pay close attention and remove them from the pan immediately.

## STORING GLUTEN-FREE VEGAN BAKED GOODS

Gluten-free baked goods taste best the day they are made. Some may stay fresh at room temperature, and others will keep in the refrigerator for a day or two. However, many factors can affect freshness; for example, in a humid climate, muffins may stay tender and cookies may become too soft. That's why I recommend immediately freezing any leftovers unless the recipe indicates otherwise. When you store baked goods in the freezer, you always have bread, muffins, and other delectables within easy reach.

After baking, cooling, and, if applicable, slicing, wrap goods in plastic before placing them inside a ziplock bag or airtight container. Separate slices of bread or rows of muffins with sheets of waxed paper before storing in the freezer. To retain the best taste, I recommend defrosting breads, muffins, and other items in the microwave or on low heat in the oven unless a recipe indicates otherwise.

To freeze loaves of bread, wait until the bread cools completely, and then use a serrated or electric knife to cut each loaf into slices. Separate the individual slices with pieces of waxed paper before storing them in the freezer.

To freeze glazed quick breads, including muffins and scones, put the baked goods in the freezer on a baking sheet until the glaze has frozen. Once the glaze has hardened, remove the items from the freezer, wrap them securely, and put them back in the freezer. Thaw glazed items at room temperature. Alternatively, glaze the baked goods after they have been frozen.

## THE GLUTEN-FREE VEGAN PANTRY

So now you're ready to stock the pantry with baking supplies. Don't be startled by the long list in table 5. You don't need all of these items to get started. Add to your supplies as you're able. Over time, you'll probably even think of additional items that you'll want to have available. This is the list of essentials that I like to have on hand so that I'm always prepared for a little impromptu baking.

| TABLE 5 | Gluten-free pantry staples |
|---|---|
| **CATEGORY** | **ITEMS** |
| Baking aids | Baking powder, baking soda, cider vinegar, powdered egg replacer, xanthan gum (use guar gum if corn-free), yeast (active dry yeast and quick-rise yeast)* |
| Dried fruits, nuts, and seeds | Almonds,* apricots, chia seeds, coconut (unsweetened shredded dried), cranberries, dates, flaxseeds,* hempseeds,* nut and seed butters (almond, cashew, tahini),* peanuts, peanut butter,* pecans,* raisins, walnuts* |
| Dried herbs | Italian seasoning |
| Extracts | Almond extract, vanilla extract |
| Fats and dairy substitutes | Canola oil, chocolate chips, coconut oil, nondairy milk (shelf-stable coconut, nut, rice, or soy),* olive oil (extra-virgin), vegan buttery spread* |
| Flours, grains, and starches | Amaranth flour,* arrowroot starch, bean flours,* cornmeal, cornstarch, millet flour,* potato starch, quinoa, quinoa flour,* sorghum flour,* tapioca flour, teff flour* |
| Ground spices | Cardamom, cinnamon, cloves, garlic powder, nutmeg |
| Sugars and other sweeteners | Agave nectar, confectioners' sugar, maple syrup (pure),* molasses (blackstrap and fancy), unrefined cane sugar (such as Sucanat) |
| Other | Applesauce (unsweetened),* cocoa powder (unsweetened), silken tofu (shelf-stable)* |

*Refrigerate after opening

## Bakers' Tricks: Common Substitutions

What could be more frustrating than being all set to bake but finding your pantry short on one essential item? Table 6 offers some simple substitutions to save the day.

**TABLE 6** Substitutions using common pantry ingredients

| INGREDIENT | SUBSTITUTION |
|---|---|
| Baking powder, 1 teaspoon | Combine ½ teaspoon cream of tartar, ¼ teaspoon baking soda, and ¼ teaspoon cornstarch or potato starch. |
| Baking soda, 1/2 teaspoon | Use 2 teaspoons baking powder. |
| Cocoa powder, 1 cup | Use 1 cup gluten-free carob powder. Keep in mind that carob does not taste like chocolate; it has its own unique flavor. It also has a bonus of being caffeine-free. |
| Confectioners' sugar, 1 cup | To make a corn-free confectioners' sugar, combine 1 cup sugar and 1½ tablespoons tapioca or potato starch in a blender. Process on high speed for 1 minute. |
| Extracts | To replace 1 teaspoon of vanilla extract, use ½ of a vanilla bean. For other extracts, use 1 to 2 drops of the equivalently flavored oil. |
| Flour, self-rising, 1 cup | Combine 1 cup gluten-free flour mix, 1½ teaspoons baking powder, and ¼ teaspoon sea salt. Add ½ to 1 teaspoon xanthan gum if it is not already in the flour mix. |
| Maple syrup, pure, 1 cup | Use ½ cup maple sugar plus ¼ cup liquid, or ⅞ cup agave nectar. |
| Raisins, 1 cup | Use 1 cup of another dried fruit (chop, if necessary). To achieve a taste similar to raisins, try dried currants or chopped dates. |
| Sugar, 1 cup | Use ⅔ cup agave nectar and decrease the liquids by 2 tablespoons for every ⅔ cup. Decrease the oven temperature by 25 degrees F and increase the baking time by 5 to 10 minutes. |
| Vinegar | Use the same amount of lemon juice. |
| Yeast, 0.6-ounce cube fresh cake yeast | Use 1½ to 2 teaspoons instant yeast, or 2 to 2¼ teaspoons active dry yeast. |

## KITCHEN EQUIPMENT

I n addition to having the right ingredients, you'll want to have the necessary kitchen tools. My suggestions in table 7 can help bakers feed their addictions to appliances and gadgets with frequent trips to kitchen supply stores. Or is that just me?

**TABLE 7**  Handy kitchen tools

| THE MUST-HAVES | THE TRY-TO-HAVES | THE FUN-TO-HAVES |
| --- | --- | --- |
| Aluminum foil, muffin-cup liners, and parchment paper | Aloe vera plant (for skin burns) | Baking sheet liners (reusable, such as a Silpat) |
| Baking pans (loaf, rectangular, round, square) | Baking pans (additional shapes and varieties) | Blender (heavy-duty) |
| Cooling racks | Cookie cutters | Coffee grinder (for grinding nuts and seeds) |
| Cutting boards (at least 2) | Electric knife (excellent for slicing gluten-free bread) | Immersion blender (for convenient processing) |
| Kitchen scissors and knives (chef's knife, paring knife, and serrated knife) | Fine grater, such as a Microplane (for citrus zests and fresh ginger) | Kitchen timer (use in addition to an oven timer when baking two things at once) |
| Measuring cups (wet and dry), measuring spoons, mixing bowls | Food processor (heavy duty, 10-cup capacity or more) | Mini food processor (for quickly chopping nuts and seeds) |
| Rolling pin | Instant-read thermometer | Oil spray bottles |
| Silicone spatulas, slotted spoons, toothpicks, wire whisks, wooden spoons | Oven mitts | Pastry mat (plastic work surface with labeled inches and rounds; handy for rolling dough or using as a nonstick surface) |
| Stand mixer (heavy-duty) | Sifter or sieve (for sifting cocoa powder, confectioners' sugar, and flour) | Pizza stone |

## TABLE 8 — Measuring spoons and cups (conventional and metric)

| CONVENTIONAL MEASURE | METRIC MEASURE (exact, in milliliters) | METRIC MEASURE (standard, in milliliters) |
|---|---|---|
| ⅛ teaspoon | 0.6 | 0.5 |
| ¼ teaspoon | 1.2 | 1 |
| ½ teaspoon | 2.4 | 2 |
| 1 teaspoon | 4.7 | 5 |
| 2 teaspoons | 9.4 | 10 |
| 1 tablespoon (3 teaspoons) | 14.2 | 15 |
| ¼ cup (4 tablespoons) | 56.8 | 60 |
| ⅓ cup (5⅓ tablespoons) | 75.6 | 75 |
| ½ cup (8 tablespoons) | 113.7 | 125 |
| ⅔ cup (10⅔ tablespoons) | 151.2 | 150 |
| ¾ cup (12 tablespoons) | 170.5 | 175 |
| 1 cup (16 tablespoons) | 227.3 | 250 |
| 4½ cups | 1,022.9 | 1,000 (1 kilogram) |

## TABLE 9 — Pans (conventional and metric)

| CONVENTIONAL MEASURE (INCHES) | METRIC MEASURE (CENTIMETERS) |
|---|---|
| 8 x 2-inch round | 20 x 5-centimeter round |
| 8 x 4 x 2½-inch loaf | 20 x 11 x 7.5-centimeter loaf |
| 8 x 8-inch square | 20 x 20-centimeter square |
| 9 x 2-inch round | 22 x 5-centimeter round |
| 9 x 5 x 3-inch loaf | 22 x 12.5 x 7.5-centimeter loaf |
| 9 x 9-inch square | 22 x 22-centimeter square |
| 9 x 13-inch rectangle | 22 x 23-centimeter rectangle |
| 10 x 4½-inch tube | 25 x 11-centimeter tube |
| 10 x 15-inch rectangle | 25 x 38-centimeter rectangle |
| 11 x 17-inch rectangle | 28 x 43-centimeter rectangle |

# Quick Breads

Preheat the oven and get ready to whip up classics like biscuits, loaves, muffins, and scones in short order. Or how about something a little different, such as savory biscotti, crackers, doughnuts, or tortillas? These flavorful quick breads rely on fruits, herbs, spices, and even gluten-free beer to hit just the right note for breakfast, lunch, and dinner.

Gluten-free quick bread batters have a similar consistency to wheat-based batters, so experienced bakers will find these recipes easy to work with. True to their name, most of these breads can be ready to go in the oven in just ten minutes. Here are some tips to make the switch to gluten-free as easy as . . . muffins.

## QUICK BREAD BAKING BASICS

Try different flours and flour combinations to find the tastes that you enjoy. See table 3 (page 15) for information about substituting flours. Note that if you interchange flours, you may need to compensate with more or less liquid. If you convert conventional wheat-based recipes to gluten-free versions, you will need more liquid.

Overall, quick bread recipes are very forgiving. This means you can confidently add a little additional nondairy milk if the batter seems too dry or a little more flour if it seems too wet. Similarly, make necessary adjustments if you live at a high altitude or in a humid area. Or make modifications based on your oven (does it run hot?), other appliances and equipment, and ingredients on hand.

Here is one important note about ingredients: It is essential that leaveners—such as baking soda and baking powder—are fresh. These ingredients make quick breads light and soft. Like wheat-based batters, gluten-free batters should not be overmixed. Mix just enough to moisten the batter and leave it at that.

## Tips for Perfect Loaves and Muffins

- When making muffins, fill each cup only three-quarters full. Fill any empty muffin cups halfway with water to prevent the pan from warping.
- Spritz paper muffin-cup liners with oil before filling. This will prevent the liners from sticking to the muffins.
- Bake loaves and muffins in the center of the oven.
- Do not let loaves and muffins stay in the pan too long after baking, or they will become soggy. As soon as they are cool enough to handle, transfer them to a cooling rack to cool completely before slicing.
- Add more liquid or reduce the baking time if loaves or muffins are turning out too dry.
- To avoid overbrowning the tops of loaves and muffins, use aluminum foil to loosely tent the pan so the baked goods won't burn before the center has time to bake through. Also, make sure the pan is in the center of the oven. If the overbrowning continues, it's possible that the oven runs hot. In the future, try decreasing the temperature by 25 degrees F.

### Mess-Free Glazing

Because gluten-free batter and dough can be sticky, I recommend putting parchment paper on baking sheets for most recipes. The environmentalist in me loves to reuse the paper if I have items to glaze. Here's how: Transfer the finished baked goods to the cooling rack. Remove the used parchment paper from the baking sheet and place it under the cooling rack. Drizzle the glaze over the goods—the parchment paper will catch any mess. Leftover newspaper also works well.

## Tips for Perfect Biscuits and Scones

- Use cold fats and liquids—such as canola oil, coconut oil, nondairy milk, olive oil, vegan buttery spread, and water—when preparing biscuits and scones.

- When mixing, use a light hand and do not overwork the dough. If you work the dough too much, biscuits and scones will turn out doughy and tough.

- When cutting biscuits, cut straight down and avoid twisting the biscuit cutter. Twisting the cutter "seals" the sides, preventing the biscuits from rising properly.

- When placing biscuits and scones on the pan to rise, arrange them so they touch slightly. They will rise better.

| TABLE 10 | Troubleshooting when baking quick breads |
|---|---|
| **PROBLEM** | **POSSIBLE CAUSES AND SOLUTIONS** |
| The tops of muffins or loaves are browned, but the inside is underbaked. | The rack may not have been in the center of the oven or the oven may run hot. Next time, decrease the temperature by 25 degrees F. |
| The muffins or loaves do not rise. | The batter was overmixed, the leavener was old, or the oven temperature was set too low. |
| The muffins or loaves are dry. | They were overbaked, or there was not enough liquid. |
| The baked goods brown too quickly. | Cover the bread loosely with aluminum foil for the remaining baking time. |

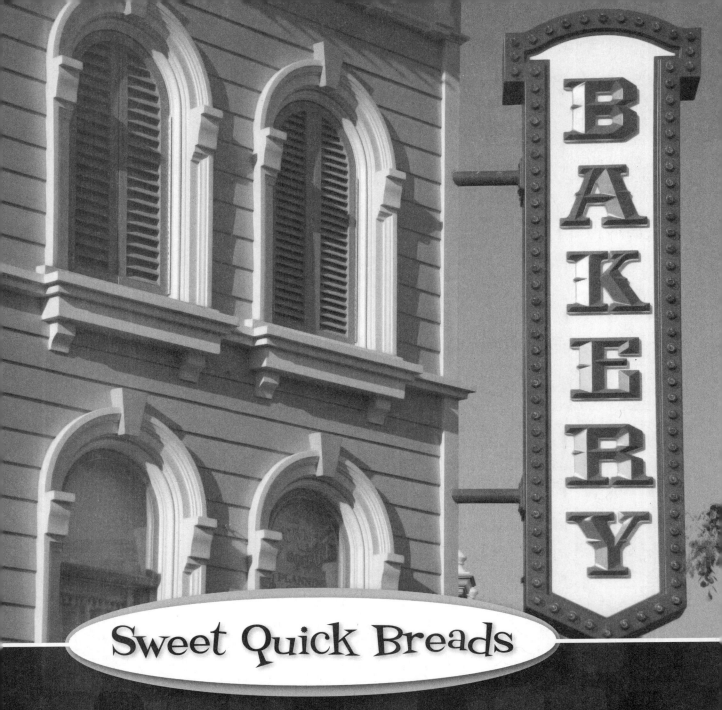

# Sweet Quick Breads

*She picked three more berries and ate them. Then she picked more berries and dropped one in the pail—kurplunk! And the rest she ate. Then Little Sal ate all four blueberries out of her pail!*

ROBERT MCCLOSKEY, *BLUEBERRIES FOR SAL*
See Wild Blueberry Scones, page 45.

Just one bite of this tender, warm loaf of banana bread, dotted with sweet chocolate chips, brings back childhood memories of after-school snack time.

# Chocolate Chip-BANANA BREAD

FREE OF: LEGUMES, NIGHTSHADES, NUTS, PEANUTS, SOY                    YIELD: 10 TO 12 SLICES

¾ cup sorghum flour

½ cup teff flour

¼ cup arrowroot starch or tapioca flour

1 tablespoon ground flaxseeds

1½ teaspoons baking soda

1½ teaspoons xanthan gum

1 teaspoon ground cinnamon

½ teaspoon sea salt

¾ cup nondairy chocolate chips

3 very ripe medium bananas, mashed (about 1½ cups)

½ cup agave nectar

3 tablespoons canola oil or coconut oil, melted

1 teaspoon vanilla extract

1 teaspoon cider vinegar

Preheat the oven to 350 degrees F. Lightly oil an 8½ x 4½-inch loaf pan.

Put the sorghum flour, teff flour, arrowroot starch, flaxseeds, baking soda, xanthan gum, cinnamon, and salt in a large bowl. Stir with a dry whisk until combined. Add the chocolate chips and stir until they are coated with the flour mixture.

Put the bananas, agave nectar, oil, vanilla extract, and vinegar in a medium bowl. Stir until well combined and smooth. Pour into the flour mixture to make a batter and stir until just moistened.

Scrape the batter into the prepared pan using a rubber spatula. Smooth out the top. Bake for 45 to 55 minutes, until a toothpick inserted in the center of the loaf comes out clean. Let cool in the pan for 10 minutes. Carefully remove the loaf from the pan and put it on a cooling rack. Let cool completely before slicing.

TIP: When bananas become very ripe, store them in the freezer, right in the peel. Remove them from the freezer about an hour before you begin baking. This way, you'll make good use for overripe bananas, and you'll be ready to make banana bread whenever the craving hits.

Per slice: calories: 311, protein: 5 g, fat: 13 g, carbohydrate: 43 g, dietary fiber: 8 g, sodium: 272 mg

Cardamom is widely known as an ingredient in Indian curries. However, in Europe it is commonly used in **sweet breads.** Ground cardamom loses its flavor quickly, so be sure to use it within a few months after opening.

# Pear-CARDAMOM BREAD

FREE OF: LEGUMES, NIGHTSHADES, NUTS, PEANUTS, SOY                    YIELD: 10 TO 12 SLICES

## BREAD

6 tablespoons unsweetened applesauce

6 tablespoons plain or vanilla nondairy milk

6 tablespoons warm water

2 tablespoons ground flaxseeds

2 tablespoons canola oil

1 teaspoon vanilla extract

1 teaspoon cider vinegar

¾ cup sorghum flour

¾ cup unrefined cane sugar

½ cup arrowroot starch

½ cup teff flour

1½ teaspoons baking powder

1½ teaspoons ground cardamom

1½ teaspoons xanthan gum

½ teaspoon sea salt

¼ teaspoon baking soda

2 ripe pears, chopped (about 1½ cups)

## TOPPING

1 tablespoon unrefined cane sugar

¼ teaspoon ground cardamom

Preheat the oven to 350 degrees F. Lightly oil an 8½ x 4½-inch loaf pan.

To make the bread, put the applesauce, nondairy milk, water, flaxseeds, oil, vanilla extract, and vinegar in a medium bowl. Stir until well combined. Let stand until thickened, about 5 minutes.

Put the sorghum flour, sugar, arrowroot starch, teff flour, baking powder, cardamom, xanthan gum, salt, and baking soda in a large bowl. Stir with a dry whisk until combined. Add the pears and toss gently until they are coated with the flour mixture.

Pour the applesauce mixture into the flour mixture to make a batter and stir until just moistened. Scrape the batter into the prepared pan using a rubber spatula. Smooth out the top.

To make the topping, put the sugar and cardamom in a small bowl. Stir until well combined. Sprinkle over the top of the unbaked loaf.

Bake for 55 to 65 minutes, until a toothpick inserted in the center of the loaf comes out clean. Let cool in the pan for 10 minutes. Carefully remove the loaf from the pan and put it on a cooling rack. Let cool completely before slicing.

**TIP:** Not everyone loves the distinctive taste of cardamom. If you don't fancy the flavor of this potent spice, use ground cinnamon instead.

**VARIATION:** Replace the pears with 2 chopped fresh peaches.

Per slice: calories: 187, protein: 3 g, fat: 4 g, carbohydrate: 36 g, dietary fiber: 3 g, sodium: 181 mg

With a deep cocoa flavor and a hint of pumpkin, a sweet slice of this loaf pairs perfectly with a mug of hot chocolate. The combination is a welcome snack for Halloween pumpkin carvers.

# COCOA-Pumpkin LOAF

FREE OF: LEGUMES,* NIGHTSHADES, NUTS, PEANUTS, SEEDS, SOY

YIELD: 10 TO 12 SLICES

1 cup sorghum flour

½ cup teff flour

¼ cup arrowroot starch

¼ cup unsweetened cocoa powder, sifted

¼ cup garfava flour or quinoa flour
(*use quinoa flour to be legume-free)

2 teaspoons baking powder

2 teaspoons ground cinnamon

2 teaspoons xanthan gum

1 teaspoon baking soda

½ teaspoon ground nutmeg

½ teaspoon sea salt

⅛ teaspoon ground cloves

1½ cups mashed cooked or canned pumpkin

½ cup agave nectar

6 tablespoons plain or vanilla nondairy milk

¼ cup unsweetened applesauce

2 tablespoons canola oil or coconut oil, melted

1 teaspoon vanilla extract

Preheat the oven to 350 degrees F. Lightly oil an 8½ x 4½-inch loaf pan.

Put the sorghum flour, teff flour, arrowroot starch, cocoa powder, garfava flour, baking powder, cinnamon, xanthan gum, baking soda, nutmeg, salt, and cloves in a large bowl. Stir with a dry whisk until combined.

Put the pumpkin, agave nectar, nondairy milk, applesauce, oil, and vanilla extract in a medium bowl. Stir until well combined. Pour into the flour mixture to make a batter and stir until just moistened.

Scrape the batter into the prepared pan using a rubber spatula. Smooth out the top. Bake for 45 to 55 minutes, until a toothpick inserted in the center of the loaf comes out clean. Let cool in the pan for 10 minutes. Carefully remove the loaf from the pan and put it on a cooling rack. Let cool completely before slicing.

Per slice: calories: 180, protein: 3 g, fat: 4 g, carbohydrate: 34 g, dietary fiber: 5 g, sodium: 285 mg

*This attractive, moist loaf is loaded with sweet potato flavor, complemented by just the right amount of cinnamon and sugar, making it perfect for brunch.*

# CINNAMON-SWIRLED Sweet Potato BREAD

FREE OF: LEGUMES,* NIGHTSHADES, NUTS, PEANUTS, SEEDS, SOY                    YIELD: 10 TO 12 SLICES

## BREAD

1 cup sorghum flour

½ cup teff flour

7 tablespoons arrowroot starch

¼ cup garfava flour or quinoa flour
(*use quinoa flour to be legume-free)

2 teaspoons baking powder

2 teaspoons ground cinnamon

2 teaspoons xanthan gum

1 teaspoon baking soda

½ teaspoon ground nutmeg

½ teaspoon sea salt

1½ cups mashed cooked sweet potato

½ cup agave nectar

6 tablespoons plain or vanilla
nondairy milk

¼ cup unsweetened applesauce

2 tablespoons canola oil or
coconut oil, melted

1 teaspoon vanilla extract

## SWIRL

3 tablespoons unrefined cane sugar

1 tablespoon ground cinnamon

Preheat the oven to 350 degrees F. Lightly oil an 8½ x 4½-inch loaf pan.

To make the bread, put the sorghum flour, teff flour, arrowroot starch, garfava flour, baking powder, cinnamon, xanthan gum, baking soda, nutmeg, and salt in a large bowl. Stir with a dry whisk until combined.

Put the sweet potato, agave nectar, nondairy milk, applesauce, oil, and vanilla extract in a medium bowl. Stir until well combined. Pour into the flour mixture to make a batter and stir until just moistened.

To make the swirl, put the sugar and cinnamon in a small bowl. Stir until well combined.

To assemble the loaf, spoon one-third of the batter into the prepared pan. Sprinkle with half of the swirl mixture. Spoon half of the remaining batter on top and sprinkle with the remaining swirl. Spoon the remaining batter over the swirl. Smooth out the top.

Bake for 45 to 55 minutes, until a toothpick inserted in the center of the loaf comes out clean. Let cool in the pan for 10 minutes. Carefully remove the loaf from the pan and put it on a cooling rack. Let cool completely before slicing.

Per slice: calories: 220, protein: 4 g, fat: 3 g, carbohydrate: 44 g, dietary fiber: 5 g, sodium: 295 mg

Quinoa makes an appearance in this hearty loaf in two ways: as a grain and a flour. This dense, **protein-packed bread** is satisfying on its own for breakfast. Or, for a real treat, use it to make french toast.

# QUINOA-RAISIN Breakfast Bread

FREE OF: LEGUMES, NIGHTSHADES, NUTS, PEANUTS, SOY

YIELD: 10 TO 12 SLICES

1 cup sorghum flour

⅔ cup unrefined cane sugar

½ cup arrowroot starch

½ cup quinoa flour

2 teaspoons baking powder

1½ teaspoons xanthan gum

1 teaspoon ground cinnamon

1 teaspoon sea salt

2 cups cooked quinoa (see sidebar)

½ cup raisins

¾ cup plus 3 tablespoons plain or vanilla nondairy milk

6 tablespoons unsweetened applesauce

2 tablespoons canola oil or coconut oil, melted

1 tablespoon ground flaxseeds

1 teaspoon vanilla extract

Preheat the oven to 350 degrees F. Lightly oil an 8½ x 4½-inch loaf pan.

Put the sorghum flour, sugar, arrowroot starch, quinoa flour, baking powder, xanthan gum, cinnamon, and salt in a large bowl. Stir with a dry whisk until combined. Stir in the quinoa and raisins until well incorporated

Put the nondairy milk, applesauce, oil, flaxseeds, and vanilla extract in a medium bowl. Stir until well combined. Pour into the flour mixture to make a batter and stir until just moistened.

Scrape the batter into the prepared pan using a rubber spatula. Smooth out the top. Bake for 45 to 55 minutes, until a toothpick inserted in the center of the loaf comes out clean. Let cool in the pan for 10 minutes. Carefully remove the loaf from the pan and put it on a cooling rack. Let cool completely before slicing.

## How to Cook Quinoa

To cook quinoa, put 1 cup of quinoa and 2 cups of water in a medium saucepan. Bring to a boil over medium heat. Decrease the heat to low, cover, and cook until the water is absorbed and the quinoa is tender, about 12 minutes. One cup of uncooked quinoa will make about 3 cups cooked.

Per slice: calories: 230, protein: 5 g, fat: 4 g, carbohydrate: 44 g, dietary fiber: 4 g, sodium: 271 mg

Serve this *classic*, sweet gingerbread on a cold winter day for breakfast or as a simple dessert.

# OLD-FASHIONED *Gingerbread*

FREE OF: LEGUMES, NIGHTSHADES, NUTS, PEANUTS, SOY
YIELD: 16 SERVINGS

Heaping ¼ cup unrefined cane sugar

¼ cup coconut oil, at room temperature

1 cup light molasses

½ cup unsweetened applesauce

1 cup hot water

1 tablespoon ground flaxseeds

1¼ cups sorghum flour

½ cup arrowroot starch

½ cup teff flour

¼ cup millet flour

2 teaspoons ground cinnamon

2 teaspoons ground ginger

2 teaspoons xanthan gum

1½ teaspoons baking soda

½ teaspoon ground cloves

½ teaspoon ground nutmeg

½ teaspoon sea salt

Preheat the oven to 350 degrees F. Lightly oil a 9-inch square baking pan.

Put the sugar and oil in a stand mixer or a large bowl. Turn the stand mixer or a hand mixer on medium speed. Beat until well combined. Beat in the molasses and applesauce until well incorporated.

Put the water in a measuring cup. Stir in the flaxseeds. Let stand until thickened, about 5 minutes.

Put the sorghum flour, arrowroot starch, teff flour, millet flour, cinnamon, ginger, xanthan gum, baking soda, cloves, nutmeg, and salt in a medium bowl. Stir with a dry whisk until combined.

Turn the mixer to low speed. Add about one-third of the flaxseed mixture and about one-third of the flour mixture to the molasses mixture, mixing well after each addition. Continue in this fashion, ending with the flour mixture, until both the flaxseed and the flour mixtures are fully incorporated into the molasses mixture to make a batter.

Scrape the batter into the prepared pan using a rubber spatula. Smooth out the top. Bake for 40 to 50 minutes, until a toothpick inserted in the center of the gingerbread comes out clean. Let cool in the pan for at least 20 minutes before serving.

Per serving: calories: 179, protein: 2 g, fat: 4 g, carbohydrate: 35 g, dietary fiber: 2 g, sodium: 194 mg

These mini-muffins come together faster than the oven preheats. They have a doughnut-like taste and texture, but without all the sugar and fat. Kid-friendly, parent approved.

# Sugarcoated MUFFIN BITES

FREE OF: NIGHTSHADES, NUTS, PEANUTS, SEEDS

YIELD: 24 MINI-MUFFINS

## MUFFIN BITES

½ cup arrowroot starch

½ cup quinoa flour

½ cup sorghum flour

2 teaspoons baking powder

1 teaspoon xanthan gum

½ teaspoon ground nutmeg

⅛ teaspoon sea salt

¾ cup vegan buttermilk (see page 17)

⅔ cup unrefined cane sugar

¼ cup unsweetened applesauce

¼ cup vegan buttery spread, melted

1 teaspoon vanilla extract

## COATING

⅓ cup confectioners' sugar, sifted

2 to 3 teaspoons ground cinnamon

Preheat the oven to 350 degrees F. Lightly coat a 24-cup mini-muffin pan with vegan buttery spread.

To make the muffin bites, put the arrowroot starch, quinoa flour, sorghum flour, baking powder, xanthan gum, nutmeg, and salt in a large bowl. Stir with a dry whisk until combined.

Put the vegan buttermilk, sugar, applesauce, vegan buttery spread, and vanilla extract in a medium bowl. Stir until well combined. Pour into the flour mixture to make a batter and stir until just moistened.

Spoon the batter into the muffin cups, filling each about three-quarters full. Bake for about 15 minutes, until a toothpick inserted in the center of a muffin comes out clean. Let the muffins cool in the pan while you prepare the coating.

To make the coating, put the confectioners' sugar and cinnamon in a small bowl. (For a more intense cinnamon flavor, add the full 3 teaspoons of cinnamon.) Stir until well combined. Carefully remove a muffin from the pan and roll it in the coating until completely covered. Place in a serving dish. Repeat with the remaining muffins. Serve warm.

**TIP:** No mini-muffin pan? No problem. This recipe makes about 10 standard-sized muffins. Bake for 16 to 20 minutes.

Per 2 muffins: calories: 123, protein: 2 g, fat: 1 g, carbohydrate: 27 g, dietary fiber: 2 g, sodium: 92 mg

These muffins were inspired by a recipe I found on a box of raisin-studded bran cereal. Pair a muffin with a protein-rich smoothie for a quick, balanced breakfast.

# BACK-OF-THE-BOX Raisin MUFFINS

FREE OF: NIGHTSHADES, NUTS, PEANUTS, SOY                    YIELD: 12 MUFFINS

3 tablespoons warm water

1 tablespoon ground flaxseeds

¾ cup sorghum flour

¼ cup garfava flour, teff flour, or buckwheat flour

¼ cup tapioca flour or arrowroot starch

1 tablespoon baking powder

1 teaspoon xanthan gum

¾ teaspoon ground cinnamon

¼ teaspoon sea salt

3 cups gluten-free vegan multigrain cereal flakes (see tip)

1¼ cups plain or vanilla nondairy milk, plus 1 to 2 tablespoons more if needed

⅓ cup raisins

⅓ cup unrefined cane sugar

¼ cup unsweetened applesauce

1½ tablespoons canola oil

Preheat the oven to 400 degrees F. Line or lightly oil a 12-cup muffin pan.

Put the water in a small bowl or measuring cup. Stir in the flaxseeds. Let stand until thickened, about 5 minutes.

Put the sorghum flour, garfava flour, tapioca flour, baking powder, xanthan gum, cinnamon, and salt in a large bowl. Stir with a dry whisk until combined.

Put the cereal in a large bowl. Stir in 1¼ cups of the nondairy milk. Let sit for at least 2 minutes, until the cereal has absorbed the nondairy milk and is soggy. Add the raisins, sugar, applesauce, oil, and flaxseed mixture. Stir until well combined. Add to the flour mixture to make a batter and stir until just moistened. If the mixture is too dry, add more nondairy milk, 1 tablespoon at a time. The batter should be thick. (Different cereals will have varying results.)

Spoon the batter into the muffin cups, filling each about three-quarters full. Bake for about 25 minutes, until a toothpick inserted in the center of a muffin comes out clean. Let cool in the pan for 5 minutes. Carefully remove the muffins from the pan and put them on a cooling rack. Let cool for at least 15 minutes before serving.

**TIP:** I recommend Nature's Path Mesa Sunrise cereal as a great choice for this recipe. Note that the ingredients do include corn and seeds and may contain traces of nuts, peanuts, and soy.

Per muffin: calories: 145, protein: 3 g, fat: 3 g, carbohydrate: 27 g, dietary fiber: 2 g, sodium: 151 mg

These **moist muffins** have just the right amount of sweetness, making them the *ideal* **breakfast** accompaniment to your favorite tofu scramble, home fries, and fresh fruit.

# Blackberry-CORNMEAL MUFFINS

FREE OF: LEGUMES, NIGHTSHADES, NUTS, PEANUTS, SEEDS, SOY

YIELD: 12 MUFFINS

1 cup whole-grain cornmeal

½ cup millet flour

½ cup sorghum flour

2 teaspoons xanthan gum

1½ teaspoons baking powder

½ teaspoon baking soda

¼ teaspoon sea salt

1 cup fresh blackberries

1 cup plus 1 tablespoon vegan buttermilk (see page 17)

1 cup unsweetened applesauce

½ cup agave nectar

2 tablespoons canola oil or coconut oil, melted

1 teaspoon vanilla extract

Preheat the oven to 325 degrees F. Line or lightly oil a 12-cup muffin pan.

Put the cornmeal, millet flour, sorghum flour, xanthan gum, baking powder, baking soda, and salt in a large bowl. Stir with a dry whisk until combined. Add the blackberries and toss gently until they are coated with the flour mixture.

Put the vegan buttermilk, applesauce, agave nectar, oil, and vanilla extract in a small bowl. Stir until well combined. Pour into the flour mixture to make a batter and stir until just moistened.

Spoon the batter into the muffin cups, filling each about three-quarters full. Bake for about 30 minutes, until lightly browned and a toothpick inserted in the center of a muffin comes out clean. Let cool in the pan for 5 minutes. Carefully remove the muffins from the pan and put them on a cooling rack. Let cool for at least 15 minutes before serving.

**VARIATION:** Instead of blackberries, substitute other berries or chopped seasonal fruits. Apples, blueberries, and peaches are among my favorites. Alternatively, leave out the fruit completely.

Per muffin: calories: 201, protein: 3 g, fat: 3 g, carbohydrate: 41 g, dietary fiber: 4 g, sodium: 171 mg

*Topped (or bottomed) with cranberries, these tender muffins taste great and look beautiful enough for holiday entertaining.*

# CRANBERRY Upside-Down MUFFINS

FREE OF: LEGUMES,* NIGHTSHADES, NUTS, PEANUTS, SOY*                    YIELD: 12 MUFFINS

## TOPPING

1½ cups fresh or frozen cranberries

¾ cup unrefined cane sugar

1 tablespoon freshly squeezed orange juice

1 tablespoon finely grated orange zest

## MUFFINS

3 tablespoons warm water

1 tablespoon ground flaxseeds

1 cup sorghum flour

½ cup quinoa flour or millet flour

½ cup tapioca flour

⅓ cup unrefined cane sugar

2 teaspoons baking powder

1½ teaspoons xanthan gum

½ teaspoon sea salt

1 cup plain or vanilla nondairy milk

¼ cup canola oil; vegan buttery spread, melted; or coconut oil, melted (*for legume- or soy-free, use canola or coconut oil)

1 teaspoon vanilla extract

Preheat the oven to 400 degrees F. Lightly oil a 12-cup muffin pan. Do not use paper liners for this recipe—the muffins will stick to the liners and make them too difficult to remove.

To make the topping, put the cranberries, sugar, orange juice, and orange zest in a medium saucepan over medium heat. Cook, stirring occasionally, until the sugar is dissolved and the cranberries begin to pop, about 10 minutes. Remove from the heat. Let stand to cool.

To make the muffins, put the water in a medium bowl. Stir in the flaxseeds. Let stand until thickened, about 5 minutes.

Put the sorghum flour, quinoa flour, tapioca flour, sugar, baking powder, xanthan gum, and salt in a large bowl. Stir with a dry whisk until combined.

Add the nondairy milk, oil, and vanilla extract to the flaxseed mixture. Stir well to combine. Pour the flaxseed mixture into the flour mixture to make a batter and stir until just moistened.

Use a spoon to evenly distribute the cranberry mixture among the prepared muffin cups. Evenly distribute the muffin batter over the cranberries in the muffin cups. Bake for 15 to 20 minutes, until lightly browned and a toothpick inserted in the center of a muffin comes out clean. Let cool in the pan for 2 minutes. Put a serving platter upside down over the pan and turn the pan and platter over together so the muffins are released onto the platter and the cranberry mixture is on top. Scoop out any cranberries that are stuck on the pan and press them onto the muffin tops. Serve warm.

Per muffin: calories: 206, protein: 3 g, fat: 6 g, carbohydrate: 37 g, dietary fiber: 2 g, sodium: 159 mg

These supermoist muffins are just plain delicious. The avocado makes them rich without adding a hint of its hue or flavor.

# Double-Chocolate MUFFINS

FREE OF: LEGUMES, NIGHTSHADES, NUTS, PEANUTS, SEEDS, SOY

YIELD: 10 TO 12 MUFFINS

½ cup plus 2 tablespoons teff flour

½ cup sorghum flour

⅓ cup unsweetened cocoa powder, sifted

¼ cup arrowroot starch

1½ teaspoons xanthan gum

1 teaspoon baking powder

½ teaspoon baking soda

½ teaspoon ground cinnamon

½ teaspoon sea salt

⅔ cup nondairy chocolate chips

1⅛ cups vegan buttermilk (see page 17)

⅔ cup unrefined cane sugar

1 small ripe avocado, flesh removed and mashed (about ⅓ cup)

1 teaspoon vanilla extract

Preheat the oven to 350 degrees F. Line or lightly oil a 12-cup muffin pan. If you use liners, brush them with oil (otherwise, these extremely soft muffins will stick to them).

Put the teff flour, sorghum flour, cocoa powder, arrowroot starch, xanthan gum, baking powder, baking soda, cinnamon, and salt in a large bowl. Stir with a dry whisk until combined. Add the chocolate chips and stir until they are coated with the flour mixture.

Pour the vegan buttermilk into a medium bowl. Add the sugar, avocado, and vanilla extract. Stir until well combined and smooth. Pour into the flour mixture to make a batter and stir until just moistened.

Spoon the batter into the muffin cups, filling each about three-quarters full. Bake for 22 to 25 minutes, until a toothpick inserted in the center of a muffin comes out clean. Let cool in the pan for 5 minutes. Carefully remove the muffins from the pan and put them on a cooling rack. Let cool for at least 15 minutes before serving. The muffins will become firmer as they stand.

**TIP:** These muffins are very tender and puddinglike in texture. Because they are so moist, they keep well and can be stored in the refrigerator for up to 2 days before freezing.

Per muffin: calories: 213, protein: 5 g, fat: 7 g, carbohydrate: 35 g, dietary fiber: 4 g, sodium: 205 mg

Here, the **classic sandwich** ingredients are combined in one delicious muffin. Feel free to use your **favorite jam or jelly** in place of my childhood mainstay, homemade strawberry jam.

# PB and J MUFFINS

FREE OF: NIGHTSHADES, NUTS, SEEDS, SOY

YIELD: 10 TO 12 MUFFINS

1 cup sorghum flour

½ cup unrefined cane sugar

½ cup teff flour

¼ cup tapioca flour

1 tablespoon baking powder

1½ teaspoons xanthan gum

½ teaspoon sea salt

1¼ cups plain or vanilla nondairy milk

½ cup natural peanut butter, smooth or chunky

¼ cup unsweetened applesauce

1 tablespoon canola oil

1 teaspoon vanilla extract

¼ to ⅓ cup strawberry jam

Preheat the oven to 400 degrees F. Line or lightly oil a 12-cup muffin pan.

Put the sorghum flour, sugar, teff flour, tapioca flour, baking powder, xanthan gum, and salt in a large bowl. Stir with a dry whisk until combined.

Put the nondairy milk, peanut butter, applesauce, oil, and vanilla extract in a medium bowl. Stir until well combined and smooth. Pour into the flour mixture to make a batter and stir until just moistened.

Spoon the batter into the muffin cups, filling each about three-quarters full. Use a small spoon to top each muffin with about 1 teaspoon of the jam. Use a wooden skewer or toothpick to swirl the jam into the batter. Bake for 20 to 25 minutes, until a toothpick inserted in the center of a muffin comes out clean. Let cool in the pan for 5 minutes. Carefully remove the muffins from the pan and put them on a cooling rack. Let cool for at least 15 minutes before serving.

**Peanut Butter and Chocolate Chip Muffins:** Omit the jam and add ½ cup of nondairy chocolate chips to the flour mixture.

Per muffin: calories: 234, protein: 7 g, fat: 7 g, carbohydrate: 36 g, dietary fiber: 3 g, sodium: 216 mg

Calcium-rich almond butter and earthy buckwheat give these easy-to-make muffins a delightful depth of flavor. Warm from the oven, they will pair nicely with your morning coffee.

# BUCKWHEAT AND Almond Butter MUFFINS

FREE OF: LEGUMES, NIGHTSHADES, PEANUTS, SEEDS, SOY                    YIELD: 10 TO 12 MUFFINS

1 cup sorghum flour

⅔ cup buckwheat flour

5 tablespoons arrowroot starch

¼ cup unrefined cane sugar

2½ teaspoons baking powder

1½ teaspoons xanthan gum

¼ teaspoon sea salt

½ cup roasted creamy almond butter

½ cup plain or vanilla nondairy milk

2 teaspoons vanilla extract

3 very ripe large bananas, mashed
(about 2 cups)

Preheat the oven to 375 degrees F. Line or lightly oil a 12-cup muffin pan.

Put the sorghum flour, buckwheat flour, arrowroot starch, sugar, baking powder, xanthan gum, and salt in a medium bowl. Stir with a dry whisk until combined.

Put the almond butter, nondairy milk, vanilla extract, and bananas in a medium bowl. Stir until well combined. Pour into the flour mixture to make a batter and stir until just moistened.

Spoon the batter into the muffin cups, filling each about three-quarters full. Bake for 19 to 22 minutes, until a toothpick inserted in the center of a muffin comes out clean. Let cool in the pan for 5 minutes. Carefully remove the muffins from the pan and put them on a cooling rack. Let cool for at least 15 minutes before serving.

**TIP:** Roasted almond butter will give these muffins a much richer flavor than raw almond butter. If you make your own almond butter, simply toast the nuts (see page 20) before you grind them.

Per muffin: calories: 203, protein: 5 g, fat: 7 g, carbohydrate: 32 g, dietary fiber: 3 g, sodium: 150 mg

This recipe is a wonderful choice for spring, when rhubarb is in season. These muffins are rich in fiber, low in fat, free of refined sugar, and so tasty you'll definitely want to pack an extra for an afternoon snack.

# BANANA-RHUBARB Crumble MUFFINS

FREE OF: NIGHTSHADES, NUTS, PEANUTS                                    YIELD: 12 MUFFINS

## MUFFINS

**1 cup sorghum flour**

**½ cup arrowroot starch**

**½ cup quinoa flour or teff flour**

**1 teaspoon baking powder**

**1 teaspoon ground cardamom**

**1 teaspoon xanthan gum**

**¾ teaspoon baking soda**

**½ teaspoon ground nutmeg**

**¼ teaspoon of sea salt**

**1½ cups diced rhubarb** (about 5 large stalks)

**3 very ripe small bananas, mashed** (about 1¼ cups)

**½ cup agave nectar**

**⅓ cup vegan buttermilk** (see page 17)

**2 tablespoons canola oil or coconut oil, melted**

**1 tablespoon ground flaxseeds**

## CRUMBLE

**¼ cup sorghum flour** (any flour will do)

**3 tablespoons unrefined cane sugar**

**1½ tablespoons vegan buttery spread, at room temperature**

Preheat the oven to 350 degrees F. Line or lightly oil a 12-cup muffin pan.

To make the muffins, put the sorghum flour, arrowroot starch, quinoa flour, baking powder, cardamom, xanthan gum, baking soda, nutmeg, and salt in a medium bowl. Stir with a dry whisk until combined. Add the rhubarb and toss until it is coated with the flour mixture.

Put the bananas, agave nectar, vegan buttermilk, oil, and flaxseeds in a large bowl. Stir well to combine. Pour into the flour mixture to make a batter and stir until just moistened.

Spoon the batter into the muffin cups, filling each about three-quarters full.

To make the crumble, put the flour and sugar in a small bowl and stir to combine. Use your fingertips to rub in the vegan buttery spread, distributing it evenly until the flour mixture resembles coarse crumbs. Sprinkle over the tops of the unbaked muffins.

Bake for 20 to 25 minutes, until golden brown and a toothpick inserted in the center of a muffin comes out clean. Let cool in the pan for 5 minutes. Carefully remove the muffins from the pan and put them on a cooling rack. Let cool for at least 15 minutes before serving.

Per muffin: calories: 206, protein: 3 g, fat: 5 g, carbohydrate: 39 g, dietary fiber: 3 g, sodium: 168 mg

This scone marries the tastes of sweet, sour, bitter, and salty. Tart raspberries complement the bitter tahini, sea salt, and sweet glaze. If you aren't a fan of tahini, use sunflower seed butter instead.

# Raspberry-TAHINI SCONES

FREE OF: LEGUMES, NIGHTSHADES, NUTS, PEANUTS, SOY                    YIELD: 6 SCONES

## SCONES

½ cup arrowroot starch

½ cup quinoa flour

½ cup sorghum flour

3 tablespoons unrefined cane sugar

2½ teaspoons baking powder

1½ teaspoons xanthan gum

½ teaspoon sea salt

6 tablespoons roasted tahini

⅓ to ⅔ cup cold plain or vanilla nondairy milk

1 cup fresh raspberries

## GLAZE

⅔ cup confectioners' sugar, sifted

3 to 5 teaspoons plain or vanilla nondairy milk

½ teaspoon vanilla extract

Preheat the oven to 400 degrees F. Line a baking sheet with parchment paper.

To make the scones, put the arrowroot starch, quinoa flour, sorghum flour, sugar, baking powder, xanthan gum, and salt in a large bowl. Stir with a dry whisk until combined.

Cut in the tahini using a pastry blender or two knives, until the mixture resembles coarse crumbs. Stir in just enough nondairy milk to make a dough. Gently stir in the raspberries.

Using floured hands, gather the dough into a cohesive ball and transfer to the lined baking sheet. Gently knead the dough two or three times until it holds together. Pat into a ½-inch-thick circle. Using a floured knife, cut the dough into 6 wedges, pulling them apart only slightly.

Bake for 18 to 22 minutes, until lightly browned. Transfer to a cooling rack and let cool for 5 minutes while you prepare the glaze.

To make the glaze, put the confectioners' sugar in a small bowl. Add 2 teaspoons of the nondairy milk and the vanilla extract. Stir, adding additional nondairy milk as needed to make a runny glaze. Drizzle over the scones. Serve warm.

**TIP:** When opening a new jar of tahini, stir in the natural oil that separates out and rises to the top. If you pour off the oil, the tahini will be rock hard instead of creamy and spreadable.

Per scone: calories: 297, protein: 6 g, fat: 9 g, carbohydrate: 46 g, dietary fiber: 5 g, sodium: 356 mg

The sweetness of apple and the spiciness of chai unite in this irresistible scone. Whip up a batch in no time for an impromptu afternoon tea with friends.

# Apple-Chai SCONES

FREE OF: NIGHTSHADES, NUTS, PEANUTS, SEEDS

YIELD: 4 SCONES

## SCONES

½ cup sorghum flour

¼ cup tapioca flour

¼ cup teff flour

3 tablespoons unrefined cane sugar

2 teaspoons baking powder

1 teaspoon xanthan gum

¼ teaspoon ground cardamom

¼ teaspoon ground cinnamon

¼ teaspoon ground ginger

¼ teaspoon sea salt

⅛ teaspoon ground cloves

⅛ teaspoon freshly ground pepper

3 tablespoons cold vegan buttery spread

1 small apple, diced (about ¾ cup)

2 to 3 tablespoons cold plain nondairy milk

## TOPPING

2 teaspoons plain nondairy milk

Ground cinnamon

Unrefined cane sugar

Preheat the oven to 425 degrees F. Line a baking sheet with parchment paper.

To make the scones, put the sorghum flour, tapioca flour, teff flour, sugar, baking powder, xanthan gum, cardamom, cinnamon, ginger, salt, cloves, and pepper in a large bowl. Using a pastry cutter or two knives, cut in the vegan buttery spread until the mixture resembles coarse crumbs. Stir in the apple.

Slowly pour the nondairy milk into the flour mixture to make a dough and stir until just moistened. Using floured hands, gather the dough into a cohesive ball and transfer to the lined baking sheet. Gently knead the dough two or three times until it holds together. Pat into a ½-inch-thick circle. Using a floured knife, cut the dough into 4 wedges, pulling them apart only slightly.

For the topping, brush the unbaked scones with the non-dairy milk. Sprinkle with cinnamon and sugar to taste.

Bake for 15 minutes, until lightly browned. Transfer to a cooling rack and let cool for at least 5 minutes. Serve warm.

Per scone: calories: 273, protein: 6 g, fat: 8 g, carbohydrate: 44 g, dietary fiber: 5 g, sodium: 414 mg

Try to use **wild blueberries** for these scones if you can find them. Supersweet and tiny, the berries give a **burst of flavor** with every bite.

# WILD Blueberry SCONES

FREE OF: NIGHTSHADES, NUTS, PEANUTS, SEEDS

YIELD: 4 SCONES

½ cup quinoa flour

½ cup sorghum flour

¼ cup arrowroot starch

2 tablespoons unrefined cane sugar

2 teaspoons baking powder

¾ teaspoon xanthan gum

⅛ teaspoon sea salt

3 tablespoons cold vegan buttery spread

1 cup wild or regular blueberries

Grated zest of 1 lemon

Juice of ½ lemon

¼ cup very cold water

Preheat the oven to 425 degrees F. Line a baking sheet with parchment paper.

Put the quinoa flour, sorghum flour, arrowroot starch, sugar, baking powder, xanthan gum, and salt in a large bowl. Use a pastry cutter or two knives to cut in the vegan buttery spread until the mixture resembles coarse crumbs. Gently stir in the blueberries and lemon zest.

Put the lemon juice and water in a large measuring cup or small bowl. Stir to combine. Slowly pour into the flour mixture to make a dough and stir just until moistened.

Using floured hands, gather the dough into a cohesive ball and transfer to the lined baking sheet. Gently knead the dough two or three times until it holds together. Pat into a ½-inch-thick circle. Using a floured knife, cut the dough into 4 wedges, pulling them apart only slightly.

Bake for 18 to 22 minutes, until lightly browned. Transfer to a cooling rack and let cool for at least 5 minutes. Serve warm.

Per scone: calories: 263, protein: 4 g, fat: 8 g, carbohydrate: 43 g, dietary fiber: 7 g, sodium: 320 mg

These scones are special enough for a *Sunday brunch,* with a sweetness that appeals to all ages. I like to add a little extra sea salt to impart a sweet-and-salty taste.

# Chocolate Chip SCONES

FREE OF: NIGHTSHADES, NUTS, PEANUTS, SEEDS

YIELD: 4 SCONES

½ cup sorghum flour

¼ cup quinoa flour

¼ cup tapioca flour

2 tablespoons unrefined cane sugar

1¼ teaspoons baking powder

½ teaspoon xanthan gum

¼ teaspoon baking soda

⅛ teaspoon sea salt

3 tablespoons cold vegan buttery spread

¼ to ⅓ cup nondairy chocolate chips

3 to 5 tablespoons cold vegan buttermilk (see page 17)

Preheat the oven to 400 degrees F. Line a baking sheet with parchment paper.

Put the sorghum flour, quinoa flour, tapioca flour, sugar, baking powder, xanthan gum, baking soda, and salt in a large bowl. Stir with a dry whisk until combined. Using a pastry cutter or two knives, cut in the vegan buttery spread until the mixture resembles coarse crumbs. Stir in the chocolate chips (use the larger amount for a more chocolaty taste).

Pour the vegan buttermilk into the flour mixture to make a dough and stir until just moistened. Using floured hands, gather the dough into a cohesive ball and transfer to the lined baking sheet. Gently knead the dough two or three times until it holds together. Pat into a ½-inch-thick circle. Using a floured knife, cut the dough into 4 wedges, pulling them apart only slightly.

Bake for 15 to 18 minutes, until lightly browned. Transfer to a cooling rack and let cool for at least 5 minutes. Serve warm.

Per scone: calories: 268, protein: 4 g, fat: 11 g, carbohydrate: 38 g, dietary fiber: 2 g, sodium: 332 mg

Nothing says **fresh-baked goodness** like rolled biscuits straight from the oven. Quicker to make than cinnamon rolls, these sweet biscuits are sure to **please everyone** at the breakfast table.

# GOOEY Maple-Pumpkin BISCUITS

FREE OF: LEGUMES, NIGHTSHADES, PEANUTS, SEEDS, SOY

YIELD: 8 BISCUITS

## TOPPING

½ cup pure maple syrup

Juice from ½ orange

## BISCUITS

1 cup sorghum flour

½ cup teff flour

¼ cup arrowroot starch

¼ cup tapioca flour, plus more for dusting and rolling

1 tablespoon baking powder

2 teaspoons xanthan gum

1 teaspoon baking soda

½ teaspoon sea salt

¾ cup mashed cooked or canned pumpkin

½ cup plain or vanilla nondairy milk

3 tablespoons canola oil or coconut oil, melted

1 tablespoon pure maple syrup

2 teaspoons vanilla extract

## FILLING

3 tablespoons unrefined cane sugar

1 teaspoon ground cinnamon

½ cup raisins

⅓ cup coarsely chopped pecans

Preheat the oven to 375 degrees F. Dust a large sheet of parchment paper with tapioca flour and set aside.

To make the topping, put the maple syrup and orange juice in an 8-inch round baking pan. Stir to combine. Set aside.

To make the biscuits, put the sorghum flour, teff flour, arrowroot starch, tapioca flour, baking powder, xanthan gum, baking soda, and salt in a large bowl. Stir with a dry whisk until combined.

Put the pumpkin, nondairy milk, oil, syrup, and vanilla extract in a medium bowl. Stir until well combined. Pour into the flour mixture to make a dough and stir until just moistened. Scrape the dough onto the prepared parchment paper using a rubber spatula. Using a lightly floured rolling pin, roll the dough into a rectangle, about 8 x 15 inches.

To make the filling, put the sugar and cinnamon in a small bowl and stir until well combined. Sprinkle over the dough, leaving a 1-inch margin at the top. Sprinkle the raisins and pecans evenly over the sugar mixture. Starting from the 15-inch side, roll the dough away from you, cinnamon-roll style (because the dough is sticky, use the parchment paper to help in this process).

Using a sharp, floured knife, slice the dough into 8 equal portions. Put each slice, cut-side down, in the prepared pan on top of the orange juice mixture.

Bake for about 30 minutes, until the biscuits have risen and are lightly browned. Let cool in the pan for 5 minutes. Put a serving platter upside down over the pan and turn the pan and platter over together so the biscuits are released onto the platter. Scrape any remaining sticky sauce from the pan over the biscuits. Serve warm.

**TIP:** If you love a buttery taste, use vegan buttery spread instead of the oil. Be sure to use soy-free vegan buttery spread if you want this recipe to be soy-free.

**VARIATION:** Replace the raisins with dried cranberries and the pecans with walnuts.

Per biscuit: calories: 260, protein: 5 g, fat: 10 g, carbohydrate: 51 g, dietary fiber: 5 g, sodium: 439 mg

*Chock-full of flavor, these biscuits pair wholesome ingredients with a sticky topping. Simple to prepare, they are sure to become a family favorite.*

# Sticky Almond BREAKFAST BISCUITS

FREE OF: NIGHTSHADES, PEANUTS

YIELD: 6 BISCUITS

## SAUCE

½ cup agave nectar

½ cup plain or vanilla nondairy milk

2 tablespoons light molasses

1 tablespoon roasted creamy almond butter

⅛ teaspoon sea salt

¾ cup coarsely chopped almonds

1 teaspoon vanilla extract

## BISCUITS

1 cup sorghum flour

½ cup quinoa flour or millet flour

½ cup tapioca flour

2 tablespoons unrefined cane sugar

1 tablespoon baking powder

1 tablespoon ground flaxseeds

1½ teaspoons xanthan gum

¼ teaspoon baking soda

⅛ teaspoon sea salt

2 tablespoons coconut oil or vegan buttery spread, at room temperature

6 tablespoons unsweetened applesauce

4 to 6 tablespoons vegan buttermilk (see page 17)

Preheat the oven to 400 degrees F. Lightly coat an 8-inch round baking pan with coconut oil or vegan buttery spread.

To make the sauce, put the agave nectar, nondairy milk, molasses, almond butter, and salt in a saucepan. Bring to a boil over medium heat. Cook, stirring often, until thickened, about 5 minutes. Once the sauce has thickened, remove it from the heat. Stir in the almonds and vanilla extract.

To make the biscuits, put the sorghum flour, quinoa flour, tapioca flour, sugar, baking powder, flaxseeds, xanthan gum, baking soda, and salt in a large bowl. Stir with a dry whisk until combined. Use your fingertips to rub in the oil, distributing it evenly until the flour mixture resembles coarse crumbs.

Add the applesauce and 4 tablespoons of the nondairy milk to the flour mixture. Stir until well combined. Stir in just enough additional nondairy milk to create a soft dough. Use a rubber spatula to scrape the dough onto a clean, lightly floured work surface. Gently knead the dough two to three times until it holds together.

Scrape the sauce into the prepared pan using a rubber spatula. Smooth out the top.

Divide the dough into six equal portions and use your hands to drop the biscuits on top of the sauce. The biscuits should touch each other slightly. Shape them if necessary, but do not overhandle them.

Bake for 15 to 18 minutes, until the biscuits have risen and are lightly browned. Let cool in the pan for 5 minutes. Put a serving platter upside down over the pan and turn the pan and platter over together so the biscuits are released onto the platter. Scrape any remaining almond sauce from the pan over the biscuits. Serve warm.

Per biscuit: calories: 447, protein: 9 g, fat: 16 g, carbohydrate: 70 g, dietary fiber: 7 g, sodium: 346 mg

Even though these **doughnuts** are not deep-fried, they will definitely satisfy cravings for the sweet coffee-house treat. Served warm, they have an **unbeatable goodness** that will make you thankful that they're baked, so you can have two.

# MAPLE-GLAZED BAKED Doughnuts

FREE OF: LEGUMES, NIGHTSHADES, NUTS, PEANUTS, SOY                    YIELD: 6 DOUGHNUTS

## DOUGHNUTS

**3 tablespoons warm water**

**1 tablespoon ground flaxseeds**

**½ cup quinoa flour**

**½ cup sorghum flour**

**⅓ cup unrefined cane sugar**

**¼ cup arrowroot starch**

**2 teaspoons baking powder**

**1 teaspoon xanthan gum**

**½ teaspoon ground cinnamon**

**½ teaspoon ground nutmeg**

**½ teaspoon sea salt**

**⅔ cup plain or vanilla nondairy milk**

**3 tablespoons canola oil or coconut oil, melted**

**1 tablespoon pure maple syrup**

**2 teaspoons vanilla extract**

**½ teaspoon cider vinegar**

## GLAZE

**1 cup confectioners' sugar, sifted**

**3 tablespoons pure maple syrup**

**2 tablespoons plain or vanilla nondairy milk**

**1 teaspoon maple extract**

Preheat the oven to 350 degrees F. Lightly oil a doughnut pan, muffin-top pan, baking sheet, or english muffin rings. If you are using a baking sheet, form six 4-inch rings out of aluminum foil. Oil each ring, then place them on the baking sheet.

To make the doughnuts, put the water in a small bowl. Stir in the flaxseeds. Let stand until thickened, about 5 minutes.

Put the quinoa flour, sorghum flour, sugar, arrowroot starch, baking powder, xanthan gum, cinnamon, nutmeg, and salt in a large bowl. Stir with a dry whisk until combined.

Add the nondairy milk, oil, maple syrup, vanilla extract, and vinegar to the flaxseed mixture. Stir until well combined. Pour into the flour mixture to make a batter and stir until just moistened.

Spoon the batter into the prepared pan or molds, smoothing out the tops. Bake for 10 to 12 minutes, until lightly golden and a toothpick inserted near the center of a doughnut comes out clean. Remove the doughnuts from the pan immediately. Let cool on a cooling rack while you prepare the glaze.

To make the glaze, put the confectioners' sugar, maple syrup, and nondairy milk in a small saucepan. Stir to combine. Bring to a boil over medium heat. Remove from the heat. Stir in the maple extract. Let stand for 10 minutes.

Dip the top of each doughnut into the glaze, being careful not to burn your fingers. The glaze will harden as the doughnuts cool. Serve warm.

**TIP:** These doughnuts freeze very well. When reheated in the microwave, they taste like they are fresh from the bakery.

Per doughnut: calories: 295, protein: 4 g, fat: 9 g, carbohydrate: 51 g, dietary fiber: 3 g, sodium: 314 mg

# Savory Quick Breads

A nickel will get you on the subway, but garlic will get you a seat.

OLD NEW YORK PROVERB

See Olive Oil Biscuits with Roasted Garlic, Rosemary, and Hempseeds, page 64

Every baker has a favorite version of **soda bread.** Popular variations include the addition of raisins or caraway seeds. This recipe is left as an open canvas for your own experimentation. The bread is **soft and crusty,** making it an easy and tasty complement to a fall soup or stew.

# SIMPLE Soda BREAD

FREE OF: LEGUMES, NIGHTSHADES, PEANUTS, SOY

YIELD: 6 TO 8 WEDGES

Whole-grain cornmeal, for the pan

3 tablespoons warm water

1 tablespoon ground flaxseeds

1 cup sorghum flour

½ cup tapioca flour

½ cup teff flour

2 tablespoons finely ground almonds

2 teaspoons xanthan gum

1 teaspoon baking powder

1 teaspoon baking soda

½ teaspoon sea salt

1 cup vegan buttermilk (see page 17)

1 tablespoon agave nectar

Preheat the oven to 375 degrees F. Lightly oil a 9-inch round baking pan. Sprinkle with cornmeal.

Put the water in a small bowl. Stir in the flaxseeds. Let stand until thickened, about 5 minutes.

Put the sorghum flour, tapioca flour, teff flour, almonds, xanthan gum, baking powder, baking soda, and salt in a large bowl. Stir with a dry whisk until combined.

Add the vegan buttermilk and agave nectar to the thickened flaxseed mixture. Stir to combine. Pour into the flour mixture to make a dough and stir until just combined.

Use floured hands to transfer the dough to the prepared pan. Pat into a circle about 7 inches in diameter. Using a sharp, lightly floured knife, score the top of the dough with an "X," cutting into the dough about 1 inch. Be careful not to cut all the way through.

Bake for 40 to 45 minutes, until lightly browned and a toothpick inserted in the center of the bread comes out clean. The bread will also sound hollow when tapped.

Transfer to a cooling rack to cool for 10 minutes before serving. Use an electric or serrated knife to slice into wedges. Serve warm.

**TIP:** Like most soda breads (not just gluten-free ones), Simple Soda Bread tastes best warm, so serve it immediately. Use any leftovers to make croutons or breadcrumbs.

Per wedge: calories: 190, protein: 6 g, fat: 3 g, carbohydrate: 36 g, dietary fiber: 5 g, sodium: 402 mg

This **easy loaf** satisfies the craving for fresh-out-of-the-oven **bliss.** Many gluten-free beers are now available; try experimenting to see which one you like best.

# Hearty BEER BREAD

FREE OF: LEGUMES,* NUTS, PEANUTS, SEEDS, SOY*                              YIELD: 10 TO 12 SLICES

1¾ cups sorghum flour

½ cup potato starch

½ cup quinoa flour

¼ cup tapioca flour

2 tablespoons unrefined cane sugar

1 tablespoon plus 1 teaspoon baking powder

1 tablespoon xanthan gum

1½ teaspoons sea salt

1 bottle (12 ounces) **gluten-free vegan beer**

2 tablespoons water

3 tablespoons vegan buttery spread, melted (*optional, omit for legume- and soy-free)

Preheat the oven to 375 degrees F. Lightly oil an 8½ x 4½-inch loaf pan.

Put the sorghum flour, potato starch, quinoa flour, tapioca flour, sugar, baking powder, xanthan gum, and salt in a large bowl. Stir with a dry whisk until combined. Gradually stir in the beer and water to make a batter. Stir until just moistened.

Scrape the batter into the prepared pan using a rubber spatula. Smooth out the top. Drizzle with the vegan buttery spread if using. Bake for 45 to 50 minutes, until golden brown and a toothpick inserted in the center of the loaf comes out clean. Let cool in the pan for 10 minutes. Carefully remove the loaf from the pan and put it on a cooling rack. Let cool for at least 20 minutes before slicing.

**TIP:** Beer and other types of alcohol may appear to be vegan even though they are not. Even if the label does not list any animal-based ingredients, the manufacturing and filtration process may have entailed the use of animal-based products, such as dairy, eggs, gelatin, and isinglass (from fish bladder). Manufacturers are not required to provide this information on the product label.

Per slice: calories: 161, protein: 4 g, fat: 1 g, carbohydrate: 32 g, dietary fiber: 3 g, sodium: 429 mg

Zucchini bread can be a **sweet treat**, but my grandpa begs to differ. No vegetables, he says, will ever grace his desserts. This bread is made with Grandpa in mind, as a **savory alternative** to the classic sweet treat.

# MEDITERRANEAN Zucchini BREAD

FREE OF: LEGUMES, NIGHTSHADES, NUTS,* PEANUTS, SOY                                        YIELD: 10 SLICES

**6 tablespoons warm water**

**2 tablespoons ground flaxseeds**

**1 cup sorghum flour**

**½ cup millet flour**

**½ cup teff flour**

**2 tablespoons unrefined cane sugar**

**2 teaspoons baking powder**

**2 teaspoons xanthan gum**

**1 teaspoon dried rosemary**

**1 teaspoon dried thyme**

**½ teaspoon baking soda**

**½ teaspoon sea salt**

**¼ teaspoon garlic powder**

**½ cup walnut pieces, toasted** (see page 20; *optional, omit for nut-free)

**1 cup shredded zucchini, drained and squeezed to remove excess moisture** (about 1 medium zucchini)

**¾ cup plus 2 tablespoons vegan buttermilk** (see page 17)

**3 tablespoons extra-virgin olive oil**

Preheat the oven to 350 degrees F. Lightly oil an 8½ x 4½-inch loaf pan.

Put the water in a medium bowl. Stir in the flaxseeds. Let stand until thickened, about 5 minutes.

Put the sorghum flour, millet flour, teff flour, sugar, baking powder, xanthan gum, rosemary, thyme, baking soda, salt, and garlic powder in a large bowl. Stir with a dry whisk until combined. Add the optional walnut pieces and toss until they are coated with the flour mixture.

Add the zucchini, vegan buttermilk, and oil to the thickened flaxseed mixture. Stir until well combined. Pour into the flour mixture to make a batter and stir until just moistened.

Scrape the batter into the prepared pan using a rubber spatula. Smooth out the top. Bake for 45 to 55 minutes, until a toothpick inserted in the center of the loaf comes out clean. Let cool in the pan for 10 minutes. Carefully remove the loaf from the pan and put it on a cooling rack. Let cool completely before slicing.

**TIP:** Be sure to squeeze all the excess moisture from the zucchini or you'll end up with a soggy loaf. For the best results, put the shredded zucchini inside a cheesecloth or a few layers of paper towels and wring it out over the sink.

**Mediterranean Zucchini Bread with Sun-Dried Tomatoes and Olives:** Add ¼ cup of finely chopped sun-dried tomatoes and ¼ cup of sliced black olives to the zucchini mixture.

Per slice: calories: 205, protein: 6 g, fat: 10 g, carbohydrate: 26 g, dietary fiber: 4 g, sodium: 256 mg

Teetering between **sweet and savory**, this bread combines the deep flavor of molasses with **wholesome ingredients.** It is especially delicious when topped with nut butter. I love toasting thick slices and generously slathering them with roasted almond butter for a perfect post-run refueling.

# MILLET-Molasses BREAD

FREE OF: LEGUMES, NIGHTSHADES, NUTS, PEANUTS, SOY          YIELD: 10 SLICES

1½ cups unsweetened nondairy milk

2 tablespoons cider vinegar

1¼ cups millet flour

1¼ cups sorghum flour

½ cup arrowroot starch

2 tablespoons ground flaxseeds

1 tablespoon xanthan gum

1 teaspoon baking soda

1 teaspoon sea salt

½ cup light molasses

Preheat the oven to 325 degrees F. Lightly oil an 8½ x 4½-inch loaf pan.

Pour the nondairy milk into a small bowl. Stir in the vinegar. Let stand until curdled, about 2 minutes.

Put the millet flour, sorghum flour, arrowroot starch, flaxseeds, xanthan gum, baking soda, and salt in a large bowl. Stir with a dry whisk until combined.

Add the molasses to the curdled nondairy milk. Stir until well combined. Pour into the flour mixture to make a batter and stir until just moistened.

Scrape the batter into the prepared pan using a rubber spatula. Smooth out the top. Bake for 45 to 55 minutes, until a toothpick inserted in the center of the loaf comes out clean. Let cool in the pan for 10 minutes. Carefully remove the loaf from the pan and put it on a cooling rack. Let cool for at least 20 minutes before slicing.

Per slice: calories: 211, protein: 6 g, fat: 2 g, carbohydrate: 44 g, dietary fiber: 4 g, sodium: 362 mg

With a **hint of maple**, this cornbread is just sweet enough to make it a dinner-worthy **sidekick** to spicy chilis and stews. It is also ideal for a holiday stuffing (see Cornbread and Wild Rice Stuffing with Apples and Pecans, page 69).

# Maple-Kissed CORNBREAD

FREE OF: LEGUMES, NIGHTSHADES, NUTS, PEANUTS, SEEDS, SOY                    YIELD: 9 SQUARES

1¼ cups whole-grain cornmeal

¾ cup sorghum flour

¼ cup arrowroot starch

1 tablespoon baking powder

1½ teaspoons xanthan gum

½ teaspoon sea salt

1½ cups unsweetened nondairy milk

⅓ cup pure maple syrup

2½ tablespoons canola oil

Preheat the oven to 350 degrees F. Lightly oil a 9-inch square glass baking dish.

Put the cornmeal, sorghum flour, arrowroot starch, baking powder, xanthan gum, and salt in a medium bowl. Stir with a dry whisk until combined.

Put the nondairy milk, maple syrup, and oil in a small bowl. Stir until well combined. Pour into the flour mixture to make a batter and stir until just moistened.

Scrape the batter into the prepared pan using a rubber spatula. Smooth out the top. Bake for 25 to 30 minutes, until a toothpick inserted in the center of the loaf comes out clean. Let cool for at least 5 minutes. Serve warm, directly from the dish.

**TIP:** If you bake this bread earlier in the day and want to serve it warm for dinner, simply preheat the oven to 250 degrees F and pop it in the oven to reheat for about 8 minutes.

Per square: calories: 201, protein: 4 g, fat: 6 g, carbohydrate: 33 g, dietary fiber: 3 g, sodium: 264 mg

A cross between creamy polenta and cornbread, this smooth bread features fresh corn and is dotted with fragrant basil. Use in-season corn, cut straight from the cob, for the best flavor.

# SWEET CORN AND BASIL Spoon Bread

FREE OF: NIGHTSHADES, NUTS, PEANUTS, SEEDS                    YIELD: 9 SERVINGS

**2 tablespoons vegan buttery spread,
plus more for the pan**

**6 ears fresh corn, kernels removed**

**¾ cup unsweetened nondairy milk**

**6 tablespoons unsweetened applesauce**

**½ cup masa harina** (see tip)

**½ teaspoon sea salt**

**5 tablespoons whole-grain cornmeal**

**2 tablespoons unrefined cane sugar**

**¾ teaspoon baking powder**

**¼ cup lightly packed fresh basil,
finely chopped**

Preheat the oven to 350 degrees F. Lightly coat a 9-inch square baking dish with vegan buttery spread.

Put 1 tablespoon of the vegan buttery spread and the corn in a medium skillet. Cook on medium-high heat, stirring occasionally, until the kernels begin to brown, 8 to 10 minutes. Transfer about 2 cups of the kernels to a food processor. Add the nondairy milk and applesauce. Process just until the corn is in small pieces (the mixture should not be smooth). Add the masa harina, salt, and remaining tablespoon of vegan buttery spread. Resume processing just until all the ingredients are incorporated.

Put the cornmeal, sugar, and baking powder in a medium bowl. Stir with a dry whisk until combined. Use a rubber spatula to scrape the corn mixture from the food processor into the bowl. Stir until smooth to make a batter. Stir in the remaining corn and the basil until well incorporated.

Scrape the batter into the prepared pan using the rubber spatula. Smooth out the top. Cover tightly with aluminum foil. Bake for 30 minutes. Remove the foil. Continue baking for 20 to 30 minutes, until the top is firm and the sides are lightly browned. Let stand for 10 minutes before serving. Serve warm, directly from the dish.

**TIP:** For the best results, use a high-quality masa harina, such as Maseca brand.

Per serving: calories: 184, protein: 5 g, fat: 4 g, carbohydrate: 33 g, dietary fiber: 4 g, sodium: 178 mg

True to their name, these crackers take no time at all to throw together. If you prefer softer crackers, simply make them a little thicker and cut the baking time by about five minutes.

# In-a-Pinch POLENTA CRACKERS

FREE OF: LEGUMES, NIGHTSHADES, NUTS, PEANUTS, SEEDS, SOY

YIELD: 36 TO 48 CRACKERS

2 cups water

¼ teaspoon sea salt

1 cup whole-grain cornmeal

2 tablespoon extra-virgin olive oil

1 teaspoon italian seasoning

⅛ teaspoon garlic powder

⅛ teaspoon onion powder

Preheat the oven to 375 degrees F. Generously coat a large baking sheet with olive oil. (Do not use parchment paper or the crackers will take longer to bake and turn out soft.)

Put the water and salt in a large saucepan. Bring to a boil over high heat. Decrease the heat to medium-low and slowly add the cornmeal, whisking constantly. Continue to cook, stirring often, until the mixture is thick and creamy, with the consistency of porridge. Remove from the heat. Stir in the oil, italian seasoning, garlic powder, and onion powder. Taste and add more salt if necessary.

Use a rubber spatula to scrape the mixture onto the prepared baking sheet. Spread thinly, about ⅛-inch thick, occasionally dipping the spatula in warm water to keep the mixture from sticking to it. Use a dull knife to score the mixture into 36 to 48 pieces.

Bake for about 30 minutes, until crispy and brown. (Thicker crackers will take longer to bake and get crisp.) Let cool completely on the pan. Break into crackers. Stored in an airtight container or ziplock bags, In-a-Pinch Polenta Crackers will keep for 3 days at room temperature or for 3 months in the freezer.

**TIP:** Try mixing up the spices, exchanging Italian flavors for Mexican (chili powder, cumin), Indian (curry powder), or French (herbes de provence).

Per 3 crackers: calories: 48, protein: 1 g, fat: 2 g, carbohydrate: 6 g, dietary fiber: 1 g, sodium: 41 mg

These are the only animals you'll find in this book. Nutritional yeast imparts the characteristic cheesy flavor in these bite-sized crackers, which are surely destined to swim in your soup.

# CHEEZY Animal CRACKERS

FREE OF: NUTS, PEANUTS, SEEDS, SOY

YIELD: 60 TO 70 CRACKERS

½ cup sorghum flour

⅓ cup nutritional yeast flakes

¼ cup arrowroot starch, plus more if needed

¼ cup garfava flour

1 teaspoon xanthan gum

½ teaspoon paprika

½ teaspoon sea salt

¼ teaspoon baking soda

¼ teaspoon onion powder

¼ cup canola oil

¼ cup water

¾ teaspoon cider vinegar

½ teaspoon agave nectar

Unsweetened nondairy milk, for brushing

Sea salt, for sprinkling

Preheat the oven to 375 degrees F. Line a baking sheet with parchment paper. Lightly oil the parchment paper.

Put the sorghum flour, nutritional yeast flakes, arrowroot starch, garfava flour, xanthan gum, paprika, salt, baking soda, and onion powder in a medium bowl. Stir with a dry whisk until combined.

Put the oil, water, vinegar, and agave nectar in a small bowl. Stir until well combined. Pour into the flour mixture to make a dough and stir until well combined.

Use a rubber spatula to scrape the dough onto a clean, lightly floured work surface. Knead about five times, to create a soft dough. If the dough is very sticky, add a bit of arrowroot starch, a little at a time, until a soft dough is formed.

Using a lightly floured rolling pin, roll the dough about ⅛-inch thick. Use small animal cookie cutters (or any other small cookie cutters) to cut out the crackers. Use a metal spatula to transfer each one onto the lined baking sheet. Continue to re-roll scraps and cut shapes until all the dough has been used.

Brush the crackers with nondairy milk. Sprinkle with salt. Bake for about 10 minutes, until lightly golden. Stored in an airtight container or ziplock bags, Cheezy Animal Crackers will keep for 3 days at room temperature or for 3 months in the freezer.

## TIPS

- Add ¼ teaspoon of ground turmeric to give more color to Cheezy Animal Crackers. They will more closely resemble their nonvegan counterparts.
- To make a trail mix, toss with dried fruit, nuts, and seeds.

Per 6 crackers: calories: 102, protein: 2 g, fat: 6 g, carbohydrate: 6 g, dietary fiber: 2 g, sodium: 132 mg

These crackers have a hint of **nuttiness** and can stand up to thick dips, making them an ideal **accompaniment** for guacamole or hummus.

# Crunchy AMARANTH CRACKERS

FREE OF: LEGUMES, PEANUTS, NUTS, SOY                                    YIELD: 15 TO 18 CRACKERS

½ cup amaranth flour

¼ cup potato starch

2 teaspoons italian seasoning

1 teaspoon garlic powder

½ teaspoon sea salt

½ teaspoon xanthan gum

¼ teaspoon baking soda

2 tablespoons unsweetened nondairy milk, plus more if needed

2 tablespoons canola oil

1 tablespoon agave nectar

½ teaspoon cider vinegar

3 tablespoons sesame seeds, toasted (see page 20)

Preheat the oven to 350 degrees F. Line a baking sheet with parchment paper.

Put the amaranth flour, potato starch, italian seasoning, garlic powder, salt, xanthan gum, and baking soda in a large bowl. Stir with a dry whisk until combined.

Put the nondairy milk, oil, agave nectar, and vinegar in a small bowl. Stir until well combined. Pour into the flour mixture and stir until a dough comes together. If the dough is too crumbly, add additional nondairy milk, a little at a time. The dough should be firm but smooth. Stir in the sesame seeds.

Use a rubber spatula to scrape the dough onto a clean, lightly floured work surface. Using a floured rolling pin, roll the dough about ⅛-inch thick. Use a 2-inch round biscuit or cookie cutter to cut out the crackers. Use a metal spatula to transfer each one to the lined baking sheet. Continue to reroll scraps and cut shapes until all the dough has been used.

Bake for about 12 minutes, until golden. Use the metal spatula to flip the crackers, then bake for about 5 more minutes, until crisp. Let cool on the pan for 5 minutes. Transfer the crackers to a cooling rack to cool completely. Stored in an airtight container or ziplock bags, Crunchy Amaranth Crackers will keep for 5 days at room temperature or for 3 months in the freezer.

Per 3 crackers: calories: 160, protein: 3 g, fat: 8 g, carbohydrate: 18 g, dietary fiber: 3 g, sodium: 263 mg

I was **snacking** on these crackers when I was out of town, riding a subway. A woman seated beside me asked if these crisps are similar to those of a popular (nongluten-free) brand. I said yes; in fact, they were my inspiration for the recipe. She asked if mine were gluten-free, saying that her niece has celiac disease. It made me smile to think of the **connections** we can make in the most unexpected situations.

# FRUIT AND NUT Crisps

FREE OF: NIGHTSHADES, PEANUTS, SOY          YIELD: 28 TO 32 CRISPS

¾ cup chickpea flour

½ cup millet flour

¼ cup hempseeds

3 tablespoons ground flaxseeds

1 tablespoon dried thyme, rubbed between your fingertips

1¼ teaspoons baking soda

1 teaspoon sea salt

¾ teaspoon xanthan gum

1 cup vegan buttermilk (see page 17)

3 tablespoons pure maple syrup

½ cup finely chopped pecans

¼ cup raisins

¼ cup dried cranberries (or additional raisins)

Preheat the oven to 350 degrees F. Lightly oil an 8 x 4-inch loaf pan.

Put the chickpea flour, millet flour, hempseeds, flaxseeds, thyme, baking soda, salt, and xanthan gum in a large bowl. Stir with a dry whisk until combined.

Put the vegan buttermilk and maple syrup in a small bowl. Stir until well combined. Pour into the flour mixture to make a batter and stir until well combined. Add the pecans, raisins, and cranberries. Stir until evenly distributed.

Scrape the batter into the prepared pan using a rubber spatula. Smooth out the top. Bake for 35 minutes, until a toothpick inserted in the center of the loaf comes out clean. Let cool in the pan for 10 minutes. Carefully remove the loaf from the pan and put it on a cooling rack. Let cool completely (this will take 1 to 2 hours).

Once the loaf has cooled, preheat the oven to 300 degrees F. Using a sharp, serrated knife or an electric knife, cut the loaf into slices, about ¼-inch thick. Consistent thickness is important for even baking.

Put the slices cut-side down on a baking sheet. Bake for 12 to 15 minutes, until toasted. Carefully flip the slices and continue baking for 12 to 15 minutes, until crisp. Let cool completely on the pan. Stored in an airtight container or ziplock bags, Fruit and Nut Crisps will keep for 4 days at room temperature or for 3 months in the freezer.

**TIP:** An electric knife is a great investment. Because gluten-free and vegan baked goods can be delicate, the knife makes slicing breads and loaves a lot easier and cleaner. For under $25, you can pick one up at a local housewares store.

Per 2 crisps: calories: 108, protein: 4 g, fat: 4 g, carbohydrate: 12 g, dietary fiber: 2 g, sodium: 260 mg

This savory biscotti goes great alongside a dinner of noodles, lentils, and sauerkraut. More tender than traditional biscotti, Peppercorn-Rye Biscotti is soft in the center like a breadstick but has a deliciously crispy exterior.

# PEPPERCORN-Rye BISCOTTI

FREE OF: LEGUMES, NUTS, PEANUTS

YIELD: 12 TO 15 BISCOTTI

½ cup sorghum flour

½ cup teff flour

¼ cup potato starch

Grated zest of 1 small orange

1 tablespoon unsweetened cocoa powder, sifted

1 tablespoon unrefined cane sugar

1¼ teaspoons baking powder

1 teaspoon xanthan gum

1 to 3 teaspoons black peppercorns, crushed

2 teaspoons caraway seeds

½ teaspoon sea salt

6 tablespoons unsweetened applesauce

3 tablespoons water

2 tablespoons canola oil

2 teaspoons blackstrap molasses

Preheat the oven to 350 degrees F. Line a baking sheet with parchment paper.

Put the sorghum flour, teff flour, potato starch, orange zest, cocoa powder, sugar, baking powder, xanthan gum, peppercorns, caraway seeds, and salt in a large bowl. (Use the larger amount of crushed peppercorns for a more peppery taste.) Stir with a dry whisk until combined.

Put the applesauce, water, oil, and molasses in a small bowl. Stir until well combined. Pour into the flour mixture to make a dough and stir until well combined.

Using lightly floured hands, transfer the dough to the lined baking sheet. Form into a log, about 10 x 3 inches. Bake for 25 minutes. Let cool on the baking sheet for at least 10 minutes.

Decrease the oven temperature to 325 degrees F. Carefully transfer the log to a cutting board. Using a sharp, serrated knife or an electric knife, cut the log into ¾-inch slices on the diagonal. Put the slices cut-side down on the lined baking sheet. Bake for 10 minutes, until toasted. Carefully flip the slices and continue baking for 10 minutes, until crisp. Transfer to a cooling rack. Let cool for at least 10 minutes before serving.

**VARIATION:** Peppercorns have a spicy kick that some people find undesirable or intolerable. If pepper doesn't agree with your taste buds, simply omit the peppercorns.

Per biscotti: calories: 82, protein: 2 g, fat: 3 g, carbohydrate: 14 g, dietary fiber: 2 g, sodium: 121 mg

My favorite **root vegetable** shines in these tender and slightly sweet drop biscuits. If you are using leftover sweet potatoes, these biscuits can be in the oven before you even decide what else you're making for dinner. *Serve warm* with vegan buttery spread.

# SWEET POTATO AND Buckwheat BISCUITS

FREE OF: NIGHTSHADES, NUTS, PEANUTS, SEEDS

YIELD: 6 BISCUITS

½ cup buckwheat flour

⅓ cup sorghum flour

¼ cup arrowroot starch

2 tablespoons unrefined cane sugar

1 tablespoon baking powder

1 teaspoon ground nutmeg

1 teaspoon xanthan gum

½ teaspoon sea salt

2 tablespoons cold vegan buttery spread

1 cup mashed cooked sweet potatoes, cooled

2 tablespoons cold unsweetened nondairy milk, plus more if needed

Preheat the oven to 425 degrees F. Line a baking sheet with parchment paper.

Put the buckwheat flour, sorghum flour, arrowroot starch, sugar, baking powder, nutmeg, xanthan gum, and salt in a large bowl. Stir with a dry whisk until combined.

Using a pastry blender or two knives, cut in the vegan buttery spread until the mixture resembles coarse crumbs. Add the sweet potatoes and 2 tablespoons of the nondairy milk to make a dough. Stir until well combined. Add additional nondairy milk, a little at a time, if the dough is too dry.

Divide the dough into six equal portions to make the biscuits. Use your hands to drop the biscuits onto the lined baking sheet. Bake for 12 to 15 minutes, until golden brown. Transfer to a cooling rack. Let cool for 5 minutes. Serve warm.

**TIPS**

- To make the biscuits less sweet, use only 1 tablespoon of unrefined cane sugar.
- Omit the nutmeg and use your favorite spices to create different flavors—chili powder and curry are two delicious options.
- If you are using leftover sweet potatoes that are seasoned with salt, decrease the amount of salt in the recipe.

Per biscuit: calories: 206, protein: 4 g, fat: 4 g, carbohydrate: 41 g, dietary fiber: 5 g, sodium: 278 mg

Round out a classic Southern breakfast with a batch of these biscuits and your favorite gravy. With their undeniable flakiness, Basic "Buttermilk" Biscuits will likely make regular appearances at your breakfast *and* dinner table.

# Basic "BUTTERMILK" BISCUITS

FREE OF: NIGHTSHADES, NUTS, PEANUTS, SEEDS

YIELD: 12 BISCUITS

1 cup amaranth flour or sorghum flour

½ cup arrowroot starch or cornstarch

½ cup tapioca flour

1¼ tablespoons baking powder

1½ teaspoons xanthan gum

½ teaspoon sea salt

¼ teaspoon baking soda

6 tablespoons cold vegan buttery spread

⅔ to ¾ cup cold vegan buttermilk (see page 17)

Preheat the oven to 450 degrees F. Line a baking sheet with parchment paper.

Put the amaranth flour, arrowroot starch, tapioca flour, baking powder, xanthan gum, salt, and baking soda in a large bowl. Stir with a dry whisk until combined.

Using a pastry blender or two knives, cut in the vegan buttery spread until the mixture resembles coarse crumbs. Gradually stir in the vegan buttermilk, a little at a time, just until a dough comes together. Use a rubber spatula to scrape the dough onto a clean, lightly floured work surface. Knead about four times, to create a soft dough.

Pat into a ½-inch thick circle. Use a biscuit cutter or large cookie cutter to cut out the biscuits, being sure to cut straight down, without twisting the cutter. Reuse the scraps and continue to cut out biscuits until all the dough has been used.

Put the biscuits on the lined baking sheet. Bake for 13 to 15 minutes, until lightly browned. Transfer to a cooling rack. Let cool for 5 minutes. Serve warm.

**Herbed Biscuits:** Add 2 tablespoons of minced fresh chives and 1 tablespoon of minced fresh dill to the flour mixture.

Per biscuit: calories: 124, protein: 2 g, fat: 5 g, carbohydrate: 17 g, dietary fiber: 2 g, sodium: 205 mg

The mellow flavor of **roasted garlic** gives these biscuits a buttery richness, the olive oil adds flakiness, and the hempseeds supply a **bit of crunch.** Garlic lovers, these melt-in-your-mouth biscuits are for you.

# Olive Oil Biscuits WITH ROASTED GARLIC, ROSEMARY, AND HEMPSEEDS

FREE OF: LEGUMES, NIGHTSHADES, NUTS, PEANUTS, SOY                    YIELD: 6 BISCUITS

**1 bulb fresh garlic**

**½ cup arrowroot starch**

**½ cup millet flour**

**½ cup sorghum flour**

**2 tablespoons unrefined cane sugar**

**1 tablespoon baking powder**

**1½ teaspoons xanthan gum**

**1 teaspoon dried rosemary, rubbed between your fingertips**

**2 tablespoons cold extra-virgin olive oil**

**⅓ to ⅔ cup cold vegan buttermilk (see page 17)**

**3 tablespoons hempseeds**

Preheat the oven to 425 degrees F. Line a baking sheet with parchment paper.

To roast the garlic, use a sharp knife to cut a thin slice off the top of the bulb, slightly exposing each clove. Wrap the bulb in aluminum foil. Bake for 40 minutes. Remove and let stand for 10 minutes. Keep the oven at 425 degrees F.

Unwrap the garlic, being careful not to burn yourself. Let cool for an additional 10 minutes. Extract the roasted garlic by squeezing the pulp into a small bowl. Use a fork to mash the garlic into a paste.

Put the arrowroot starch, millet flour, sorghum flour, sugar, baking powder, xanthan gum, and rosemary in a large bowl. Stir with a dry whisk until combined. Use a fork to stir in the oil until it is evenly distributed and the flour mixture is crumbly. Gradually stir in the vegan buttermilk, a little at a time, just until a dough comes together.

Use a spatula to scrape the dough onto a clean, lightly floured work surface. Knead about three times, until a soft dough is formed. Divide the dough into six equal portions to make the biscuits. Use your hands to drop the biscuits onto the lined baking sheet. Equally distribute the garlic on top of each biscuit. Sprinkle with the hempseeds.

Bake for 15 to 20 minutes, until golden brown. Transfer to a cooling rack. Let cool for 5 minutes. Serve warm.

**TIP:** Hempseeds pack a nutritional punch of protein and omega-3 fatty acids. However, if you don't have them on hand, use finely chopped walnuts or a sprinkling of sunflower seeds instead.

Per biscuit: calories: 228, protein: 7 g, fat: 8 g, carbohydrate: 34 g, dietary fiber: 3 g, sodium: 194 mg

The addition of nutritional yeast flakes gives these biscuits a **cheesy, nutty** taste without a hint of dairy. It also provides **protein** and many nutrients, including vitamin $B_{12}$.

# Easy Cheezy DINNER BISCUITS

FREE OF: NIGHTSHADES, NUTS, PEANUTS, SEEDS

YIELD: 12 BISCUITS

**1 cup sorghum flour**

**⅓ cup nutritional yeast flakes**

**⅓ cup quinoa flour or millet flour**

**⅓ cup tapioca flour**

**5 teaspoons baking powder**

**2 teaspoons italian seasoning**

**1¼ teaspoons xanthan gum**

**½ teaspoon sea salt**

**5 tablespoons cold vegan buttery spread**

**½ to ¾ cup cold vegan buttermilk** (see page 17)

Preheat the oven to 450 degrees F. Lightly oil or line a baking sheet with parchment paper.

Put the sorghum flour, nutritional yeast flakes, quinoa flour, tapioca flour, baking powder, italian seasoning, xanthan gum, and salt in a large bowl. Stir with a dry whisk until combined.

Using a pastry blender or two knives, cut in the vegan buttery spread until the mixture resembles coarse crumbs. Gradually stir in the vegan buttermilk, a little at a time, just until a dough comes together.

Use a spatula to scrape the dough onto a clean, lightly floured work surface. Pat into a ½-inch-thick circle. Use a biscuit cutter or large cookie cutter to cut out the biscuits, being sure to cut straight down, without twisting the cutter. Reuse the scraps and continue to cut out biscuits until all the dough has been used.

Put the biscuits on the prepared baking sheet. Bake for 13 to 15 minutes, until lightly browned. Transfer to a cooling rack. Let cool for 5 minutes. Serve warm.

Per biscuit: calories: 110, protein: 3 g, fat: 5 g, carbohydrate: 15 g, dietary fiber: 2 g, sodium: 281 mg

Jalapeño and red pepper give these scones color and a **Southwestern flair.** Avocado provides a healthful fat, perfectly complementing the Tex-Mex flavors and boosting nutrition. For a savory brunch, serve Spicy Southwest Scones alongside chili or a tofu scramble, with **fresh salsa.**

# SPICY *Southwest* SCONES

FREE OF: LEGUMES, NUTS, PEANUTS, SEEDS, SOY

YIELD: 8 SCONES

¾ cup sorghum flour

½ cup arrowroot starch

½ cup whole-grain cornmeal

1 tablespoon unrefined cane sugar

2 teaspoons baking powder

1½ teaspoons xanthan gum

1 teaspoon chili powder

½ teaspoon ground cumin

½ teaspoon sea salt

1 large ripe avocado, flesh removed and mashed

3 tablespoons finely chopped sweet red pepper

1 to 2 tablespoons seeded, finely chopped jalapeño chile

⅓ to ½ cup cold vegan buttermilk (see page 17)

Preheat the oven to 400 degrees F. Line a baking sheet with parchment paper.

Put the sorghum flour, arrowroot starch, cornmeal, sugar, baking powder, xanthan gum, chili powder, cumin, and salt in a large bowl. Stir with a dry whisk until combined.

Add the avocado to the flour mixture. Stir until well combined and the mixture resembles coarse crumbs. Stir in the red pepper and chile. Gradually stir in the vegan buttermilk, a little at a time, just until a dough comes together.

Use a spatula to scrape the dough onto the lined baking sheet. Knead about five times, to create a soft dough. Pat into a ½-inch-thick circle. Using a floured knife, cut the dough into 8 wedges, pulling them apart only slightly.

Bake for 23 to 28 minutes, until lightly browned. Transfer to a cooling rack. Let cool for 5 minutes. Serve warm.

**TIP:** For a delicious crunch, sprinkle the scones with 2 to 3 tablespoons of *pepitas* (hulled pumpkin seeds) before baking.

Per scone: calories: 155, protein: 4 g, fat: 5 g, carbohydrate: 24 g, dietary fiber: 5 g, sodium: 416 mg

These **easy-to-prepare** tortillas are handy for **quick lunches.** Fill them with black beans, spicy salsa, crisp lettuce, and vegan sour cream.

# BUCKWHEAT Tortillas

FREE OF: LEGUMES, NIGHTSHADES, NUTS, PEANUTS, SEEDS, SOY

YIELD: 6 TORTILLAS

⅓ cup buckwheat flour, plus more if needed

⅓ cup sorghum flour

⅓ cup tapioca flour, plus more for rolling

¾ teaspoon xanthan gum

½ teaspoon baking powder

¼ teaspoon sea salt

½ cup hot water

1 to 2 teaspoons canola oil, as needed

Put the buckwheat flour, sorghum flour, tapioca flour, xanthan gum, baking powder, and salt in a large bowl. Stir with a dry whisk until combined. Gradually add the water, stirring until well combined. If needed, add additional buckwheat flour, a little at a time, to create a soft dough that is not sticky.

Divide the dough into six equal portions. Roll each portion between your palms to form a ball. Sprinkle a sheet of waxed paper with tapioca flour. Put a ball of dough on the waxed paper. Using a lightly floured rolling pin, roll the dough as thinly as possible without tearing it to make a tortilla.

Heat 1 teaspoon of the oil in a large nonstick skillet over medium-high heat. Carefully use the waxed paper to invert the tortilla onto the skillet. Cook for about 2 minutes, until lightly browned on the bottom. Use a heat-resistant spatula to carefully flip the tortilla over. Cook the other side for 2 minutes, until lightly browned. Transfer the tortilla to a plate. Cover with a clean dish towel to keep warm. Repeat with the remaining balls of dough, adding additional oil to the skillet as needed. Serve warm.

Per tortilla: calories: 78, protein: 2 g, fat: 2 g, carbohydrate: 15 g, dietary fiber: 1 g, sodium: 119 mg

Bannock is a traditional, flat quick bread that is also known as fry bread. There are many ways to serve it: split like an english muffin, stuffed to make a breakfast sandwich, doused in pure maple syrup, topped with fresh jam, or slathered with vegan buttery spread.

# CHICKPEA Bannock (FRY BREAD)

FREE OF: NIGHTSHADES, NUTS, PEANUTS, SEEDS, SOY

YIELD: 3 OR 4 BANNOCKS

1 cup chickpea flour

1 tablespoon baking powder

1 tablespoon unrefined cane sugar

1 teaspoon xanthan gum

¼ teaspoon sea salt

½ cup room-temperature water, as needed

Put the chickpea flour, baking powder, sugar, xanthan gum, and salt in a large bowl. Stir with a dry whisk until combined. Gradually stir in just enough of the water to create a soft dough.

Using lightly floured hands, form the dough into three or four ¾-inch-thick patties. Lightly coat a nonstick skillet with canola oil and heat over medium heat.

Put the patties in the skillet, being careful not to crowd them. Cook over medium heat for about 5 minutes, until browned on the bottom. Use a heat-resistant spatula to carefully flip each patty over. Continue cooking for about 5 minutes, until heated through and browned on the other side. Serve warm.

Per bannock: calories: 120, protein: 6 g, fat: 2 g, carbohydrate: 17 g, dietary fiber: 4 g, sodium: 481 mg

This **nontraditional stuffing** is made from **homemade cornbread**, nutty wild rice, crunchy pecans, and sweet apples. If you prepare the cornbread and rice in advance, the stuffing can be made in no time.

# CORNBREAD AND Wild Rice Stuffing
## WITH APPLES AND PECANS

FREE OF: LEGUMES,* NIGHTSHADES, PEANUTS, SEEDS, SOY*

YIELD: 9 SERVINGS

2½ cups vegetable or mushroom broth

2 cups water

1 cup wild rice

4 tablespoons extra-virgin olive oil, or
1 tablespoon extra-virgin olive oil plus 3 tablespoons vegan buttery spread, melted
(*for legume- and soy-free, use olive oil)

2 small onions, finely chopped

2 celery stalks, finely chopped

3 tablespoons chopped fresh parsley

1 tablespoon chopped fresh thyme

2 garlic cloves, minced

1 teaspoon ground sage

1 teaspoon sea salt, plus more if needed

¼ teaspoon freshly ground pepper, plus more if needed

5 cups crumbled Maple-Kissed Cornbread (page 55)

1 cup pecans, toasted (see page 20)

2 large apples, coarsely chopped (about 2 cups)

Preheat the oven to 375 F. Lightly oil a 9 x 11-inch baking dish.

Put 2 cups of the broth, the water, and the rice in a saucepan over medium heat. Bring to a simmer, cover, and cook until tender, about 40 minutes. Remove from the heat. Let stand, covered, for 20 minutes. Use a rubber spatula to scrape the rice (including any leftover liquid) into the prepared baking dish.

Heat 1 tablespoon of the oil in a large skillet over medium heat. Add the onion and celery and cook, stirring occasionally, until softened. Stir in the parsley, thyme, garlic, sage, salt, and pepper. Cook until fragrant, 1 to 2 minutes.

Add the onion mixture to the rice. Stir until well combined. Add the cornbread, pecans, and apples. Mix until well combined. Drizzle with the remaining ½ cup of broth and 3 tablespoons of oil. Season with additional salt and pepper to taste.

Bake for about 30 minutes, until the top is browned and crisp and the apples are tender. Serve warm.

Per serving: calories: 403, protein: 7 g, fat: 21 g, carbohydrate: 46 g, dietary fiber: 6 g, sodium: 530 mg

# Yeast Breads

Freshly baked sweet and savory yeast breads have a goodness that just can't be beat. From proofing the yeast to savoring your first bite, nothing is more rewarding than baking yeast breads from scratch. Still, some people find the prospect a little daunting, and making gluten-free yeast bread may seem like an even bigger challenge. It's true that baking with yeast is a less forgiving process than making quick breads. However, if you take your time and are careful not to forget an ingredient or skip a step, you'll soon master gluten-free bagels, breads, buns, and rolls, not to mention flatbread, fritters, pita bread, and pizza crust.

## YEAST BREAD BAKING BASICS

Cooks who are used to making wheat-based batter will see differences when they work with gluten-free ingredients. Gluten-free bread dough is naturally more sticky and moist than wheat-based bread dough. It's similar to a thick muffin batter, but not as thick as cookie dough, and very shiny. Oil your hands when you handle the dough; this helps to control the stickiness. Avoid using too much flour when you work the dough or you may end up with a heavy, dense bread.

When you make gluten-free yeast breads, try different flours and flour combinations to find the tastes you most enjoy. Flours with a high protein content give a better structure to baked goods, so choose amaranth, quinoa, sorghum, and teff flours over rice flour. (See table 3, page 15, for more information about flours.) Note that if you interchange flours, you may need to compensate with more or less liquid. If you convert conventional wheat-based recipes to gluten-free versions, you will need more liquid. Here are two important points to keep in mind when you make yeast breads: (1) bring all the ingredients to room temperature before you start, and (2) be sure all the ingredients, including the yeast, are fresh.

Yeast is a living organism (as a fungus, it is appropriate for a vegan diet). When it is activated, yeast creates carbon dioxide gas, which is the critical rising agent for baking breads. There are three types of yeast:

- Active dry yeast, which is available in ¼ ounce packets or jars, is dormant. You can test active dry yeast to make sure it is alive before baking. This process is called "proofing." To proof active dry yeast, add 1 teaspoon of sugar to ¼ cup of warm water (about 110 degrees F). Stir in one envelope of yeast (2¼ teaspoons) and let it stand for ten minutes. If the yeast foams at least ½ inch, it is active.

- Quick-rise yeast, which is also known as instant yeast or bread machine yeast, comes in smaller granules than active dry yeast and doesn't need to be proofed. In recipes, quick-rise yeast is often added directly to the flour mixture.

- Fresh yeast, which is also known as compressed or cake yeast, is found in the refrigerated section of the grocery store. It needs to be proofed in tepid water (80 degrees F), without sugar.

A 0.6-ounce cube of fresh cake yeast is roughly equivalent to 1½ to 2 teaspoons of quick-rise yeast or 2 to 2¼ teaspoons of active dry yeast. To substitute quick-rise yeast for active dry yeast, use 25 percent less quick-rise yeast.

Once opened, all yeast varieties should be stored in the refrigerator. Fresh yeast will spoil within a few weeks, while active dry and quick-rise yeasts can be used until the expiration date.

Your oven and environmental factors may affect the quality of yeast breads. You will need to make adjustments to a recipe or the baking time if you live at a high altitude or in a humid area, or if your oven runs hot. If there are children in your household, discourage them from jumping up and down in front of the oven if you've put the bread inside to rise.

As with quick breads, do not let yeast breads stay in the pan too long after baking, or they will become soggy. As soon as they are cool enough to handle, transfer them to a cooling rack to cool. Let loaves cool completely before slicing. Let most other baked goods cool for at least twenty minutes.

## Tips for Using the Right Equipment

- Invest in a heavy-duty stand mixer. This is a significant but worthwhile expense because electric hand mixers often cannot handle thick, gluten-free dough. I offer hand mixers as an alternative to stand mixers in my recipes; however, hand mixers may not hold up to frequent use.

- Use the paddle attachment—not the dough hook—on the stand mixer for making gluten-free breads.

- Use a rubber spatula to scrape down the sides of the bowl after adding the dry ingredients to the wet ingredients. This is an important step before beating the dough.

- Use a timer. If the recipe says to beat the mixture for five minutes, set the timer and beat the mixture for five minutes. Do not estimate. This step kneads and aerates the dough, which is necessary for the bread to rise properly.

- When in doubt, use a slightly larger pan. Unlike wheat-based dough, gluten-free dough will spill over the sides of the pan if it rises higher than the edges.

- Preheat the oven for longer than you think may be necessary. Most ovens need at least ten minutes to preheat to the correct temperature. Some ovens have a second chime that indicates when they are truly preheated.

- Bake yeast breads in the center of the oven.

- Invest in an instant-read thermometer, which is instrumental in determining whether yeast breads are done baking (see below).

### Testing for Doneness

An instant-read thermometer can help you determine whether yeast bread is done baking. Insert the thermometer in the center of the loaf, away from the bottom and sides of the pan. A fully baked loaf should register 200 degrees F (100 degrees C). The device is also handy for determining the temperature of the liquid when proofing yeast. Instant-read thermometers are available for less than $10 at any housewares store.

If you don't have an instant-read thermometer, there are other ways to test yeast bread for doneness. These include inserting a toothpick in the middle of the loaf to see if it comes out clean, and tapping on the bottom of the loaf, which should produce a hollow sound.

## Tips for Rising Yeast Breads

- Always let yeast breads rise uncovered in a warm, draft-free place. I prefer to preheat the oven when I start prepping the ingredients, shutting it off after about three minutes, and putting the dough inside to rise. In the warm oven, the dough will rise beautifully—and often more quickly than the recipe indicates. The only exceptions are pita bread and pizza crust, because the baking pan or pizza stone has to preheat on its own for a long time before the bread or crust are baked.

- If you find the dough is not rising adequately, remember this trick when baking the next batch: replace the liquid in the recipe with club soda or gluten-free beer. The carbonation will help the dough rise.

- Be sure that the dough doesn't overrise. If it rises above the pan, too much air will enter the dough, and the bread will collapse during baking.

- If you are making shaped breads, such as bagels or buns, shape them with oiled hands before rising. Let them rise uncovered in a warm, draft-free place until doubled in size, then bake as directed. Let shaped breads rise only once, even if you are adapting a conventional recipe that has two or three rising times.

**TABLE 11** — Troubleshooting when baking yeast breads

| PROBLEM | POSSIBLE CAUSES AND SOLUTIONS |
|---|---|
| The bread never rises. | The dough was too dry, or the yeast may have been dead. |
| The bread rises then falls. | There was too much liquid in the dough, or the bread was underbaked. |
| The bread browns too quickly. | Cover the bread loosely with aluminum foil for the remaining baking time. |
| The bread has a gummy center. | The dough was too wet, there was too much xanthan gum, the ingredients were not mixed well, or the bread simply didn't finish baking. |
| The bread is crumbly. | The dough was too dry, there was not enough xanthan gum, or there was not enough fat. |
| The bread turns out like a brick. | The ingredients were not mixed well. |

# Sweet Yeast Breads

*Memory is a way of holding onto the things you love,
the things you are, the things you never want to lose.*

KEVIN ARNOLD, *THE WONDER YEARS*

See Grandma's Polish Babka, page 78.

This tender loaf is sweetened with pure maple syrup. I love to use it as a base for french toast, which I suggest serving with additional syrup.

# Maple-RAISIN BREAD

FREE OF: LEGUMES, NIGHTSHADES, PEANUTS, SOY                    YIELD: 15 TO 20 SLICES

1 cup warm water

2½ teaspoons active dry yeast

1 teaspoon unrefined
cane sugar

2½ tablespoons ground
flaxseeds

1 cup sorghum flour

½ cup quinoa flour

⅓ cup tapioca flour

¼ cup finely ground almonds

¼ cup millet flour

1 tablespoon xanthan gum

1 teaspoon sea salt

⅓ cup pure maple syrup

2 tablespoons canola oil

1 teaspoon vanilla extract

1 teaspoon cider vinegar

1⅓ cups raisins

Lightly oil an 8½ x 4½-inch loaf pan.

Put ½ cup of the water in a large measuring cup. Stir in the yeast and sugar. Let stand for about 5 minutes, until the yeast has bubbled and foamed about ½ inch.

Put the remaining ½ cup of water in a heavy-duty stand mixer or a large bowl. Stir in the flaxseeds. Let stand until thickened, about 5 minutes.

Put the sorghum flour, quinoa flour, tapioca flour, almonds, millet flour, xanthan gum, and salt in a medium bowl. Stir with a dry whisk until combined.

Add the maple syrup, oil, vanilla extract, and vinegar to the thickened flaxseed mixture. Using the stand mixer or a hand mixer, beat on medium speed for 1 to 2 minutes, until combined. Turn the mixer to low speed and gradually add the proofed yeast mixture and the flour mixture to make a dough. Turn off the mixer and scrape down the sides of the bowl with a rubber spatula. Resume mixing on medium-high speed for 5 minutes. Turn off the mixer. Stir in the raisins until evenly distributed. The dough will be very sticky, similar to thick muffin batter.

Scrape the dough into the prepared pan using the rubber spatula. Smooth out the top. Let the dough rise uncovered in a warm, draft-free place for about 70 minutes, just until it reaches the top of the pan.

About 10 minutes before the dough is done rising, preheat the oven to 350 degrees F. (If the dough is rising in the oven, be sure to remove it first.)

Bake for 35 to 40 minutes, until the top of the loaf is browned and a toothpick inserted in the center of the loaf comes out clean. Carefully remove the loaf from the pan and put it on a cooling rack. Let cool completely before slicing.

**Cinnamon Maple-Raisin Bread:** Add 2 teaspoons of ground cinnamon to the flour mixture.

Per slice: calories: 141, protein: 3 g, fat: 3 g, carbohydrate: 26 g, dietary fiber: 3 g, sodium: 125 mg

This earthy loaf is brimming with the taste of apple cider and has just a hint of spice. It rises high, is slightly sweet, and tastes great as a not-so-traditional sandwich bread.

# Apple Cider AND BUCKWHEAT BREAD

FREE OF: LEGUMES, NIGHTSHADES, NUTS, PEANUTS, SOY                    YIELD: 15 SLICES

¼ cup warm water

3 tablespoons plus 1 teaspoon unrefined cane sugar

1 tablespoon active dry yeast

1⅓ cups warm apple cider

2 tablespoons ground flaxseeds

1 cup plus 1 tablespoon sorghum flour

¾ cup buckwheat flour

⅓ cup arrowroot starch

¼ cup tapioca flour

2¼ teaspoons xanthan gum

1 teaspoon sea salt

¾ teaspoon ground cinnamon

¾ teaspoon ground ginger

3 tablespoons canola oil

1 teaspoon cider vinegar

½ teaspoon vanilla extract

Lightly oil an 8½ x 4½-inch loaf pan.

Put the water in a large measuring cup. Stir in 1 teaspoon of the sugar and the yeast. Let stand for about 5 minutes, until the yeast has bubbled and foamed about ½ inch.

Pour the apple cider into a heavy-duty stand mixer or a large bowl. Stir in the flaxseeds. Let stand until thickened, about 5 minutes.

Put the sorghum flour, buckwheat flour, arrowroot starch, tapioca flour, xanthan gum, salt, cinnamon, ginger, and remaining 3 tablespoons of sugar in a medium bowl. Stir with a dry whisk until combined.

Add the oil, vinegar, and vanilla extract to the thickened flaxseed mixture. Using the stand mixer or a hand mixer, beat on medium speed for 1 to 2 minutes, until combined. Turn the mixer to low speed and gradually add the proofed yeast mixture and the flour mixture to make a dough. Turn off the mixer and scrape down the sides of the bowl with a rubber spatula. Resume mixing on medium-high speed for 5 minutes. The dough will be very sticky, similar to thick muffin batter.

Scrape the dough into the prepared pan using the spatula. Smooth out the top. Let the dough rise uncovered in a warm, draft-free place for about 70 minutes, just until it reaches the top of the pan.

About 10 minutes before the dough is done rising, preheat the oven to 350 degrees F. (If the dough is rising in the oven, be sure to remove it first.)

Bake for 35 to 45 minutes, until the top of the loaf is browned and a toothpick inserted in the center of the loaf comes out clean. Carefully remove the loaf from the pan and put it on a cooling rack. Let cool completely before slicing.

Per slice: calories: 121, protein: 2 g, fat: 4 g, carbohydrate: 21 g, dietary fiber: 2 g, sodium: 144 mg

Every Easter, my **grandma** (*babcia*) baked the most delicious *babka*, a spongy **Easter bread** that is traditionally made with egg yolks and butter. This vegan, gluten-free version, which is moist and sweet, brings back **childhood memories.**

# Grandma's POLISH BABKA

FREE OF: NIGHTSHADES, PEANUTS

## BREAD

¾ cup plus 2 tablespoons warm unsweetened nondairy milk

2 tablespoons ground flaxseeds

2¼ teaspoons active dry yeast

1 teaspoon unrefined cane sugar

5 tablespoons vegan buttery spread

¼ cup agave nectar

Grated zest of 1 lemon

2 teaspoons vanilla extract

½ teaspoon ground cinnamon

½ teaspoon cider vinegar

¼ teaspoon ground nutmeg

¼ teaspoon sea salt

¼ teaspoon ground turmeric (see tips)

½ cup arrowroot starch

½ cup millet flour

½ cup quinoa flour

½ cup sorghum flour

¼ cup tapioca flour

2½ teaspoons xanthan gum

½ cup raisins

Lightly oil a 9 x 5-inch loaf pan.

To make the bread, pour the nondairy milk into a large measuring cup. Stir in the flaxseeds, yeast, and sugar. Let stand for about 5 minutes, until the yeast has bubbled and foamed about ½ inch.

Put the vegan buttery spread and agave nectar in a heavy-duty stand mixer or a large bowl. Using the stand mixer or a hand mixer, beat on medium-high speed until fluffy, about 3 minutes. Turn off the mixer and add the lemon zest, vanilla extract, cinnamon, vinegar, nutmeg, salt, and turmeric. Resume mixing on medium speed until well combined.

Put the arrowroot starch, millet flour, quinoa flour, sorghum flour, tapioca flour, and xanthan gum in a medium bowl. Stir with a dry whisk until combined.

Turn the mixer to low speed and gradually add the proofed yeast mixture and the flour mixture to the agave nectar mixture to make a dough. Turn off the mixer and scrape down the sides of the bowl with a rubber spatula. Resume mixing on medium-high speed for 5 minutes. Turn off the mixer. Stir in the raisins until evenly distributed. The dough will be very sticky, similar to thick muffin batter.

Scrape the dough into the prepared pan using the rubber spatula. Smooth out the top. Let the dough rise uncovered in a warm, draft-free place for about 70 minutes, just until it reaches the top of the pan.

Per slice: calories: 173, protein: 3 g, fat: 5 g, carbohydrate: 30 g, dietary fiber: 3 g, sodium: 72 mg

## TOPPING

**1½ tablespoons agave nectar**

**2 to 3 tablespoons finely ground almonds**

For the topping, brush the dough with the agave nectar and sprinkle with the almonds.

About 10 minutes before the dough is done rising, preheat the oven to 350 degrees F. (If the dough is rising in the oven, be sure to remove it first.)

Bake for 40 minutes. Decrease the temperature to 325 degrees F. Continue baking for 15 minutes, until the top of the loaf is browned and a toothpick inserted in the center of the loaf comes out clean. Carefully remove the loaf from the pan and put it on a cooling rack. Let cool for at least 20 minutes before slicing.

### TIPS

- In the absence of egg yolks, turmeric adds a yellowish hue to this bread. Feel free to omit it if you don't have it on hand.

- Agave nectar browns breads and other baked goods more quickly than other sweeteners. Use aluminum foil to tent the pan after about 30 minutes of baking to prevent over-browning.

A double dose of **chocolate** is accented with rich **hazelnut and coffee** flavor, giving this bread a bittersweet taste that's hard to resist.

# DOUBLE-CHOCOLATE Hazelnut BREAD

FREE OF: LEGUMES, NIGHTSHADES, PEANUTS, SOY                    YIELD: 12 TO 15 SLICES

½ cup warm brewed coffee

1 cup plus 2 tablespoons warm water

1 tablespoon ground flaxseeds

⅓ to ½ cup plus 1 teaspoon unrefined cane sugar

2½ teaspoons active dry yeast

¼ cup hazelnut butter

1 teaspoon vanilla extract

½ teaspoon cider vinegar

¾ cup sorghum flour

½ cup teff flour

⅓ cup arrowroot starch

⅓ cup unsweetened cocoa powder, sifted

¼ cup plus 1½ teaspoons tapioca flour

¼ cup quinoa flour

2½ teaspoons xanthan gum

1 teaspoon sea salt

½ teaspoon ground cinnamon

⅓ cup nondairy chocolate chips

Lightly oil a 9 x 5-inch loaf pan.

Put the coffee and ¼ cup of the water in a heavy-duty stand mixer or a large bowl. Stir in the flaxseeds. Let stand until thickened, about 5 minutes.

Put the remaining ¾ cup plus 2 tablespoons of water in a large measuring cup. Stir in 1 teaspoon of the sugar and the yeast. Let stand for about 5 minutes, until the yeast has bubbled and foamed about ½ inch.

Add the remaining ⅓ to ½ cup of sugar, hazelnut butter, vanilla extract, and vinegar to the thickened flaxseed mixture. Using the stand mixer or a hand mixer, beat on medium speed for about 1 minute, until well combined.

Put the sorghum flour, teff flour, arrowroot starch, cocoa powder, ¼ cup of the tapioca flour, quinoa flour, xanthan gum, salt, and cinnamon in a medium bowl. Stir with a dry whisk until combined.

Put the chocolate chips and remaining 1½ teaspoons of tapioca flour in a small bowl. Stir until the chocolate chips are evenly coated.

Turn the mixer to low speed and gradually add the proofed yeast mixture and the flour mixture to the hazelnut mixture to make a dough. Turn off the mixer and scrape down the sides of the bowl with a rubber spatula. Resume mixing on medium-high speed for 5 minutes. Turn off the mixer. Stir in the chocolate chips until evenly distributed. The dough will be very sticky, similar to thick muffin batter.

Scrape the dough into the prepared pan using the spatula. Smooth out the top. Let the dough rise uncovered in a warm, draft-free place for about 70 minutes, just until it reaches the top of the pan.

About 10 minutes before the dough is done rising, preheat the oven to 350 degrees F. (If the dough is rising in the oven, be sure to remove it first.)

Bake for 35 to 45 minutes, until the top of the loaf is browned and a toothpick inserted in the center of the loaf comes out clean. Carefully remove the loaf from the pan and put it on a cooling rack. Let cool for at least 20 minutes before slicing.

**Double-Chocolate Peanut Butter Bread:** Replace the hazelnut butter with natural peanut butter.

Per slice: calories: 156, protein: 3 g, fat: 5 g, carbohydrate: 26 g, dietary fiber: 4 g, sodium: 155 mg

Composed of bite-sized balls of dough, this flavorful bread has a *triple dose of coconut.* Serve it *family-style,* warm from the oven, with a fresh fruit salad, for a light breakfast.

# COCONUT Pull-Apart BREAD

FREE OF: LEGUMES, NIGHTSHADES, NUTS, PEANUTS, SOY  YIELD: 6 SERVINGS

## BREAD

⅓ cup plus 2 tablespoons warm water

⅔ cup warm coconut milk

¼ cup plus 1 teaspoon unrefined cane sugar

1 tablespoon ground flaxseeds

2½ teaspoons active dry yeast

1 cup sorghum flour

⅓ cup plus 1 tablespoon quinoa flour

⅓ cup arrowroot starch

⅓ cup tapioca flour

2 teaspoons xanthan gum

½ teaspoon sea salt

2 tablespoons unsweetened shredded dried coconut

1 tablespoon coconut oil, melted (see tip)

1 teaspoon vanilla extract

## COATING

2½ tablespoons unsweetened shredded dried coconut

2½ tablespoons unrefined cane sugar

1½ tablespoons coconut milk

Lightly oil an 8 x 4-inch loaf pan.

To make the bread, put the water and coconut milk in a large measuring cup. Stir in 1 teaspoon of the sugar, the flaxseeds, and yeast. Let stand for about 5 minutes, until the yeast has bubbled and foamed about ½ inch.

Put the sorghum flour, quinoa flour, arrowroot starch, tapioca flour, xanthan gum, and salt in a medium bowl. Stir with a dry whisk until combined.

Put the remaining ¼ cup of sugar, the coconut, oil, and vanilla extract in a heavy-duty stand mixer or a large bowl. Turn the stand mixer or a hand mixer on low speed and gradually add the flour mixture and proofed yeast mixture to make a dough. Turn off the mixer and scrape down the sides of the bowl with a rubber spatula. Resume mixing on medium-high speed for 5 minutes.

To make the coating, put the coconut and sugar in a small bowl. Stir to combine. Put the coconut milk in another small bowl.

To assemble the bread, dip a tablespoon into the coconut milk. Using the same spoon, scoop a ball of the dough from the bowl and dip it into the coconut mixture, coating it well. Transfer it to the prepared pan. Repeat until all the dough has been used. Use your fingers to gently squish the dough balls together. Top with any remaining coconut mixture. Let rise uncovered in a warm, draft-free place for about 55 minutes, until doubled in size.

About 10 minutes before the dough is done rising, preheat the oven to 350 degrees F. (If the dough is rising in the oven, be sure to remove it first.)

Bake for 25 to 30 minutes, until golden brown. Carefully remove the loaf from the pan and put it in a serving dish. Let cool for 10 minutes before serving.

**TIP:** Try using virgin coconut oil to give the bread an even more pronounced coconut flavor.

Per serving: calories: 336, protein: 5 g, fat: 14 g, carbohydrate: 50 g, dietary fiber: 5 g, sodium: 186 mg

Monkey bread, also known as **bubble bread,** is a breakfast food that could pass for dessert. Balls of **sweet dough** are coated with a cinnamon-sugar mixture to form a sticky, gooey loaf when baked. The origin of the name is unknown, but this version pays tribute to our monkey friends with the inclusion of bananas. Because this recipe uses rich nut oil instead of vegan buttery spread, it's safe for soy-free folks too.

# BANANA-NUT Monkey BREAD

FREE OF: LEGUMES, NIGHTSHADES, PEANUTS, SOY

YIELD: 8 SERVINGS

## BREAD

1⅓ cups warm water

2 tablespoons plus 1 teaspoon unrefined cane sugar

1½ tablespoons ground flaxseeds

1 tablespoon active dry yeast

1¼ cups sorghum flour

½ cup arrowroot starch

½ cup quinoa flour

¼ cup finely ground almonds

¼ cup tapioca flour

2½ teaspoons xanthan gum

1 teaspoon sea salt

2 tablespoons canola oil

2 teaspoons vanilla extract

2 teaspoons cider vinegar

## COATING

¾ cup **nuts** (such as almonds, hazelnuts, pecans, or walnuts), **toasted** (see page 20) **and chopped**

⅓ cup unrefined cane sugar

1 tablespoon ground cinnamon

3 tablespoons hazelnut oil or other nut oil

1 teaspoon vanilla extract

2 small ripe bananas, finely **chopped** (about 1 cup)

Lightly oil a 9-inch or 10-inch bundt pan.

To make the bread, put the water in a large measuring cup. Stir in 1 teaspoon of the sugar, the flaxseeds, and yeast. Let stand for about 5 minutes, until the yeast has bubbled and foamed about ½ inch.

Put the sorghum flour, arrowroot starch, quinoa flour, almonds, tapioca flour, xanthan gum, salt, and remaining 2 tablespoons of sugar in a heavy-duty stand mixer or large bowl. Stir with a dry whisk until combined.

Add the canola oil, vanilla extract, and vinegar to the proofed yeast mixture. Turn the stand mixer or a hand mixer on low speed and gradually add the yeast mixture to the flour mixture to make a dough. Turn off the mixer and scrape down the sides of the bowl with a rubber spatula. Resume mixing on medium-high speed for 4 minutes.

To make the coating, put the nuts, sugar, and cinnamon in a small bowl. Stir to combine. Put the hazelnut oil and vanilla extract in another small bowl. Stir until well combined.

To assemble the bread, dip a tablespoon into the hazelnut oil mixture. Using the same spoon, scoop a ball of dough from the bowl and dip it into the oil mixture, coating it well. Transfer it to the sugar mixture, gently turning to coat. Transfer it to the prepared pan. Repeat with the remaining dough, distributing the banana pieces among the dough balls. Use your fingers to gently squish the dough balls together. Top with any remaining sugar mixture. Let rise uncovered in a warm, draft-free place for about 55 minutes, until doubled in size.

About 10 minutes before the dough is done rising, preheat the oven to 350 degrees F. (If the dough is rising in the oven, be sure to remove it first.)

Bake for 30 to 35 minutes, until golden brown. Let cool in the pan for 5 minutes. Put a serving platter upside down over the pan and turn the pan and platter over together so the bread is released onto the platter. Serve warm.

Per serving: calories: 396, protein: 8 g, fat: 18 g, carbohydrate: 50 g, dietary fiber: 7 g, sodium: 270 mg

Because the pancake batter for this recipe is prepared the **night before**, the pancakes will practically be waiting for you in the morning. Serve them with pure maple syrup and fresh berries if you like. For an extra-blissful breakfast, stir nondairy **chocolate chips** into the batter.

# Overnight BUCKWHEAT PANCAKES

FREE OF: NIGHTSHADES, NUTS, PEANUTS

YIELD: 8 TO 10 LARGE PANCAKES

¼ cup warm water

3 teaspoons unrefined cane sugar

2½ teaspoons active dry yeast

1 cup sorghum flour

¾ cup buckwheat flour

¼ cup arrowroot starch

1 tablespoon ground flaxseeds

1 teaspoon baking powder

1 teaspoon xanthan gum

¾ teaspoon sea salt

2 cups vegan buttermilk (see page 17)

2 tablespoons vegan buttery spread, at room temperature

1 teaspoon vanilla extract

⅓ cup plain or vanilla nondairy milk (optional)

Put the water in a large measuring cup. Stir in 1 teaspoon of the sugar and the yeast. Let stand for about 5 minutes, until the yeast has bubbled and foamed about ½ inch.

Put the sorghum flour, buckwheat flour, arrowroot starch, flaxseeds, baking powder, xanthan gum, salt, and remaining 2 teaspoons of sugar in a large bowl. Stir with a dry whisk until combined.

Ad the proofed yeast mixture, vegan buttermilk, vegan buttery spread, and vanilla extract to the flour mixture to make a batter. Stir until well combined. Cover the bowl tightly with plastic wrap. Chill in the refrigerator for 8 to 12 hours.

When you are ready to cook the pancakes, add the optional nondairy milk to the batter if it has become too thick. Stir until well combined.

To cook the pancakes, lightly coat a large nonstick skillet with canola oil or vegan buttery spread and heat over medium-high heat. When the oil is hot, pour ¼ cup of the batter into the skillet for each pancake (the number of pancakes that can be cooked at a time will depend on the size of the skillet). Cook until bubbles form on the top and the edges begin to dry, about 3 minutes. Use a firm, heat-resistant spatula to carefully flip the pancakes over. Cook until golden brown on the bottom, 1 to 2 minutes. Repeat with the remaining batter. Serve warm.

Per pancake: calories: 151, protein: 6 g, fat: 4 g, carbohydrate: 24 g, dietary fiber: 3 g, sodium: 261 mg

*Tangy cranberries* pair beautifully with *buttery pecans* in these easy-to-make buns. Serve warm with a smear of homemade jam, roasted nut butter, or vegan buttery spread.

# BREAKFAST BUNS WITH Cranberries and Pecans

FREE OF: LEGUMES, NIGHTSHADES, NUTS,* PEANUTS, SOY                    YIELD: 12 BUNS

## BUNS

1½ cups warm water

2½ tablespoons ground flaxseeds

⅓ cup plus 1 teaspoon unrefined cane sugar

1 tablespoon active dry yeast

1 cup sorghum flour

½ cup quinoa flour

⅓ cup arrowroot starch

¼ cup finely ground almonds

¼ cup tapioca flour

2½ teaspoons xanthan gum

2 teaspoons ground cardamom (see tip)

1 teaspoon ground cinnamon (see tip)

1 teaspoon sea salt

½ teaspoon ground nutmeg

2 tablespoons canola oil

1 teaspoon vanilla extract

1 teaspoon cider vinegar

1½ cups fresh or frozen cranberries, coarsely chopped

1 cup pecans, coarsely chopped
(*omit for nut-free)

Lightly oil a 9-inch square pan.

To make the buns, put 1 cup of the water in a heavy-duty stand mixer or a large bowl. Stir in the flaxseeds. Let stand until thickened, about 5 minutes.

Put the remaining ½ cup of water in a large measuring cup. Stir in 1 teaspoon of the sugar and the yeast. Let stand for about 5 minutes, until the yeast has bubbled and foamed about ½ inch.

Put the sorghum flour, quinoa flour, arrowroot starch, almonds, tapioca flour, xanthan gum, cardamom, cinnamon, salt, and nutmeg in a medium bowl. Stir with a dry whisk until combined.

Add the oil, vanilla extract, and vinegar to the thickened flaxseed mixture. Using the stand mixer or a hand mixer, beat on medium speed for about 1 minute, until completely combined. Turn the mixer to low speed and gradually add the proofed yeast mixture and the flour mixture to make a dough. Turn off the mixer and scrape down the sides of the bowl with a rubber spatula. Resume mixing on medium-high speed for 5 minutes. Turn off the mixer and stir in the cranberries and pecans until evenly distributed.

To form the buns, drop the dough by heaping spoonfuls into the prepared pan. Let rise uncovered in a warm, draft-free place for about 70 minutes, until doubled in size.

Per bun: calories: 251, protein: 4 g, fat: 13 g, carbohydrate: 30 g, dietary fiber: 4 g, sodium: 180 mg

TOPPING

**3 to 5 tablespoons pure maple syrup**

**1 tablespoon unrefined cane sugar**

**1 teaspoon ground cardamom** (see tip)

About 10 minutes before the dough is done rising, preheat the oven to 350 degrees F. (If the dough is rising in the oven, be sure to remove it first.)

For the topping, gently brush the buns with maple syrup. (Use the larger amount of maple syrup for a sweeter taste.) Sprinkle evenly with sugar and cardamom.

Bake for 18 to 22 minutes, until lightly browned and a toothpick inserted in the center of a bun comes out clean. Remove from the pan immediately and transfer to a serving platter. Let cool for at least 10 minutes. Pull apart into individual buns before serving. Serve warm.

**TIP:** If you find the taste of cardamom too strong, decrease the amount to 1 teaspoon and increase the amount of cinnamon to 2 teaspoons. For the topping, use cinnamon instead of cardamom.

More **decadent** than your average cinnamon rolls, these orange-glazed swirls are infused with pumpkin and filled with rich chocolate. The combination is **undeniably delicious**.

# Chocolate-Filled PUMPKIN CINNAMON ROLLS WITH ORANGE GLAZE

FREE OF: LEGUMES, NIGHTSHADES, NUTS, PEANUTS, SOY               YIELD: 8 TO 10 ROLLS

## ROLLS

½ cup warm water

2 tablespoons plus 1 teaspoon unrefined cane sugar

2½ teaspoons active dry yeast

¾ cup mashed cooked or canned pumpkin

½ cup plus 1 tablespoon plain or vanilla nondairy milk

2 tablespoons coconut oil, melted

1 tablespoon ground flaxseeds

1 teaspoon vanilla extract

1 teaspoon cider vinegar

1¼ cups sorghum flour

½ cup arrowroot starch, plus more for rolling

½ cup millet flour

½ cup teff flour

¼ cup tapioca flour

2¼ teaspoons xanthan gum

1½ teaspoons ground cinnamon

1 teaspoon ground nutmeg

1 teaspoon sea salt

Lightly oil a 10-inch round baking pan.

To make the rolls, put the water in a large measuring cup. Stir in 1 teaspoon of the sugar and the yeast. Let stand for about 5 minutes, until the yeast has bubbled and foamed about ½ inch.

Put the pumpkin, nondairy milk, oil, flaxseeds, vanilla extract, vinegar, and remaining 2 tablespoons of sugar in a heavy-duty stand mixer or large bowl. Using the stand mixer or a hand mixer, beat on medium speed until well combined.

Put the sorghum flour, arrowroot starch, millet flour, teff flour, tapioca flour, xanthan gum, cinnamon, nutmeg, and salt in a medium bowl. Stir with a dry whisk until combined.

Turn the mixer to low speed and gradually add the proofed yeast mixture and the flour mixture to the pumpkin mixture to make a dough. Turn off the mixer and scrape down the sides of the bowl with a rubber spatula. Resume mixing on medium-high speed for 3 minutes.

Lightly oil a piece of parchment paper (18 to 20 inches long) and lightly sprinkle it with arrowroot starch. Use the spatula to scrape the dough onto the parchment paper. Top with a second piece of oiled parchment paper about the same size, with the oiled side facing the dough. Use a rolling pin to roll the dough between the pieces of parchment paper to form a 16 x 12-inch rectangle. The dough will be sticky.

Per roll: calories: 376, protein: 7 g, fat: 8 g, carbohydrate: 71 g, dietary fiber: 6 g, sodium: 247 mg

## FILLING

¼ cup unsweetened applesauce

3 tablespoons unsweetened cocoa powder, sifted

2½ tablespoons agave nectar

1 tablespoon arrowroot starch

2 teaspoons ground cinnamon

⅔ cup nondairy chocolate chips

## GLAZE

1½ cups confectioners' sugar, sifted

Grated zest of 1 orange

2 tablespoons freshly squeezed orange juice, plus more if needed

½ teaspoons vanilla extract

To make the filling, put the applesauce, cocoa powder, agave nectar, arrowroot starch, and cinnamon in a small bowl. Stir until well combined. Use the spatula to spread the filling over the dough, leaving a 1-inch border at the top. Sprinkle with the chocolate chips. Starting from the 16-inch side, roll the dough away from you, cinnamon-roll style (because the dough is sticky, use the parchment paper to help in this process).

Using a sharp, floured knife, slice the dough into 8 to 10 equal portions. Put each slice, cut-side down, in the prepared pan. Let rise uncovered in a warm, draft-free place for about 45 minutes, until doubled in size. The rolls should be touching each other and the sides of the pan.

About 10 minutes before the dough is done rising, preheat the oven to 375 degrees F. (If the dough is rising in the oven, be sure to remove it first.)

Bake for about 25 minutes, until the rolls are lightly browned. Let cool in the pan for 5 minutes. Put a serving platter upside down over the pan and turn the pan and platter over together so the rolls are released onto the platter.

To make the glaze, put the confectioners' sugar in a small bowl. Stir in the orange zest, orange juice, and vanilla extract. Add additional orange juice or water, a little at a time, to thin the glaze if necessary. Drizzle over the rolls. Serve warm.

*If you like* fluffy *yet hearty cinnamon buns, loaded with raisins and topped with a* vanilla glaze, *this recipe should be right up your alley.*

# BREAKFAST Cinnamon BUNS

FREE OF: NIGHTSHADES, NUTS, PEANUTS                                      YIELD: 8 TO 10 BUNS

## BUNS

½ cup warm water

¼ cup plus 1 teaspoon unrefined cane sugar

2½ teaspoons active dry yeast

¾ cup warm plain or vanilla nondairy milk

¼ cup vegan buttery spread, melted

1 tablespoon ground flaxseeds

1 teaspoon vanilla extract

1 teaspoon cider vinegar

1¼ cups sorghum flour

¾ cup millet flour

½ cup arrowroot starch, plus more for rolling

½ cup quinoa flour

2¼ teaspoons xanthan gum

¾ teaspoon sea salt

Lightly oil a 10-inch round baking pan.

To make the buns, put the water in a large measuring cup. Stir in 1 teaspoon of the sugar and the yeast. Let stand for about 5 minutes, until the yeast has bubbled and foamed about ½ inch.

Put the remaining ¼ cup of sugar, the nondairy milk, vegan buttery spread, flaxseeds, vanilla extract, and vinegar in a heavy-duty stand mixer or a large bowl. Using the stand mixer or a hand mixer, beat on medium-speed until well combined.

Put the sorghum flour, millet flour, arrowroot starch, quinoa flour, xanthan gum, and salt in a medium bowl. Stir with a dry whisk until combined. Turn the mixer to low speed and gradually add the proofed yeast mixture and the flour mixture to make a dough. Turn off the mixer and scrape down the sides of the bowl with a rubber spatula. Resume mixing on medium-high for 3 minutes. The dough will be sticky and thick.

Lightly oil a piece of parchment paper (18 to 20 inches long) and lightly sprinkle it with arrowroot starch. Use the spatula to scrape the dough onto the parchment paper. Top with a second piece of oiled parchment paper about the same size, with the oiled side facing the dough. Use a rolling pin to roll the dough between the pieces of parchment paper to form a 16 x 12-inch rectangle.

Per bun: calories: 388, protein: 7 g, fat: 6 g, carbohydrate: 79 g, dietary fiber: 5 g, sodium: 229 mg

## FILLING

½ cup unrefined cane sugar

2 tablespoons sorghum flour

1 tablespoon ground cinnamon

2 tablespoons unsweetened applesauce

¾ cup raisins

## GLAZE

1½ cups confectioners' sugar, sifted

2 tablespoons plain or vanilla nondairy milk, plus more if needed

1 teaspoon vanilla extract

To make the filling, put the sugar, sorghum flour, and cinnamon in a small bowl. Stir until well combined. Stir in the applesauce until well combined. Use the spatula to spread the filling over the dough, leaving a 1-inch border at the top. Sprinkle the raisins over the filling. Starting from the 16-inch side, roll the dough away from you, cinnamon-roll style (because the dough is sticky, use the parchment paper to help in this process).

Using a sharp, floured knife, slice the dough into 8 to 10 equal portions. Put each slice, cut-side down, in the prepared pan. Let rise uncovered in a warm, draft-free place for about 45 minutes, until doubled in size. The buns should be touching each other and the sides of the pan.

About 10 minutes before the dough is done rising, preheat the oven to 375 degrees F. (If the dough is rising in the oven, be sure to remove it first.)

Bake for about 30 minutes, until the buns are lightly browned. Let cool in the pan for 5 minutes. Put a serving platter upside down over the pan and turn the pan and platter over together so the rolls are released onto the platter.

To make the glaze, put the confectioners' sugar in a small bowl. Stir in the nondairy milk and vanilla extract. Add additional nondairy milk, a little at a time, to thin the glaze if necessary. Drizzle over the buns. Serve warm.

Dotted with **raisins**, these sweet, orange-flavored breadsticks make a **tasty addition** to a breakfast or brunch. To give these breadsticks a doughnutlike texture, make them a bit thicker than a traditional breadstick.

# Orange-Raisin BREADSTICKS WITH Vanilla Glaze

FREE OF: LEGUMES, NIGHTSHADES, NUTS, PEANUTS, SEEDS, SOY          YIELD: 12 TO 18 BREADSTICKS, DEPENDING ON SIZE

## BREADSTICKS

½ cup warm water, plus more if needed

3 teaspoons unrefined cane sugar

1 tablespoon active dry yeast

⅔ cup sorghum flour

½ cup millet flour

½ cup quinoa flour

½ cup tapioca flour

Grated zest and juice of 1 large orange

2 teaspoons xanthan gum

¾ teaspoon ground ginger

½ teaspoon ground nutmeg

½ teaspoon sea salt

2 tablespoons agave nectar

2 tablespoons canola oil

1½ teaspoons cider vinegar

1 teaspoon vanilla extract

½ cup raisins

Line a baking sheet with parchment paper.

To make the breadsticks, put the water in a large measuring cup. Stir in 1 teaspoon of the sugar and the yeast. Let stand for about 5 minutes, until the yeast has bubbled and foamed about ½ inch.

Put the sorghum flour, millet flour, quinoa flour, tapioca flour, orange zest, xanthan gum, ginger, nutmeg, salt, and remaining 2 teaspoons of sugar in a heavy-duty stand mixer or a large bowl. Stir with a dry whisk until combined.

Put the orange juice in a measuring cup. Add enough water to total ¾ cup.

Add the agave nectar, oil, vinegar, and vanilla extract to the proofed yeast mixture. Stir until well combined.

Turn the stand mixer or a hand mixer on low speed. Gradually add the yeast mixture and the orange juice to the flour mixture to make a dough. Turn off the mixer and scrape down the sides of the bowl with a rubber spatula. Resume mixing on medium-high speed for 4 minutes. Stir in the raisins until evenly distributed. The dough will be very sticky, similar to thick muffin batter.

Lightly oil the inside of a large ziplock plastic bag. Use scissors to snip off about 1¼ inches from the bottom corner of the bag. Alternatively, use a pastry bag with a 1¼-inch tip.

Per breadstick: calories: 140, protein: 2 g, fat: 2 g, carbohydrate: 28 g, dietary fiber: 2 g, sodium: 73 mg

GLAZE

1 cup confectioners' sugar, sifted

2 teaspoons vanilla extract

1 to 3 teaspoons plain or vanilla nondairy milk

Use the spatula to scrape the dough into the bag and then seal the bag closed. Gently squeeze the bag, piping the dough into strips, about 5 inches long, on the lined baking sheet. Leave about 1 inch between the breadsticks. Let rise uncovered in a warm, draft-free place for 40 to 60 minutes, until doubled in size.

About 10 minutes before the dough is done rising, preheat the oven to 425 degrees F. (If the dough is rising in the oven, be sure to remove it first.)

Bake for 15 to 25 minutes (thicker breadsticks will need to bake longer) until firm to the touch and lightly browned. Let cool on the baking sheet while you prepare the glaze.

To make the glaze, put the confectioners' sugar in a small bowl. Stir in the vanilla extract and nondairy milk until well combined. Add additional nondairy milk, a little at a time, to thin the glaze if necessary. Drizzle over the breadsticks. Serve warm.

You may not want to eat these deep-fried *delights* every day, but they certainly fit the bill when you crave a soft doughnut with a slightly crisp exterior and *gooey glaze.* For a more healthful version, see Maple-Glazed Baked Doughnuts (page 49).

# Deep-Fried GLAZED DOUGHNUTS

FREE OF: LEGUMES, NIGHTSHADES, PEANUTS, SOY          YIELD: ABOUT 12 LARGE DOUGHNUTS PLUS DOUGHNUT HOLES, OR 20 SMALL DOUGHNUTS

## DOUGHNUTS

⅔ cup plus 2 tablespoons warm coconut milk

3 tablespoons plus 1 teaspoon unrefined cane sugar

3 tablespoons coconut oil, melted

1 tablespoon ground flaxseeds

1 teaspoon cider vinegar

½ teaspoon vanilla extract

¼ cup warm water

1 tablespoon active dry yeast

¾ cup sorghum flour

½ cup arrowroot starch, plus more for rolling

½ cup quinoa flour

¼ cup sweet rice flour

2 tablespoons finely ground almonds

2 tablespoons millet flour

2 teaspoons baking powder

2 teaspoons xanthan gum

1½ teaspoons ground nutmeg (see tip)

½ teaspoon sea salt

4 to 8 cups vegetable oil, for frying (depending on the size of your pot)

Line a baking sheet with parchment paper.

To make the doughnuts, put the coconut milk, 3 tablespoons of the sugar, coconut oil, flaxseeds, vinegar, and vanilla extract in a heavy-duty stand mixer or a large bowl. Using the stand mixer or a hand mixer, beat on medium speed until well combined. Let stand until thickened, about 5 minutes.

Put the water in a large measuring cup. Stir in 1 teaspoon of the sugar and the yeast. Let stand for about 5 minutes, until the yeast has bubbled and foamed about ½ inch.

Put the sorghum flour, arrowroot starch, quinoa flour, sweet rice flour, almonds, millet flour, baking powder, xanthan gum, nutmeg, and salt in a medium bowl. Stir with a dry whisk until combined.

Turn the mixer to low speed and gradually add the proofed yeast mixture and the flour mixture to the coconut milk mixture to make a dough. Turn off the mixer and scrape down the sides of the bowl with a rubber spatula. Resume mixing on medium-high speed for 3 minutes. The dough will be very thick and slightly sticky.

Sprinkle additional arrowroot starch on a clean work surface. Use the spatula to scrape half of the dough onto the work surface. Use a lightly floured rolling pin to roll the dough about ¼-inch thick. Use a floured doughnut cutter or round cookie cutter to cut out doughnuts. If you are using a round cutter, use a floured finger to poke a hole in the center of the each doughnut. Transfer the doughnuts and doughnut holes (if using a doughnut cutter) to the lined baking sheet. Continue to reroll scraps and cut out doughnuts until all the dough has been used. Let rise uncovered in a warm, draft-free place for about 40 minutes, until doubled in size.

## GLAZE

**2½ cups confectioners' sugar, sifted**

**¼ cup coconut milk or plain or vanilla nondairy milk**

**1 tablespoon vanilla extract** (optional)

**1 teaspoon freshly grated orange zest** (optional)

Pour the vegetable oil into a large pot or dutch oven, at least 2 inches deep. Heat the oil to 350 degrees F (use a deep-fry thermometer to check the temperature). Using a slotted spoon, carefully slide the doughnuts into the oil. Cook three to four doughnuts at a time, depending on the size of your pot. Do not overcrowd them. Cook for about 1 minute, until the bottom is golden. Use the spoon to flip the doughnuts and continue cooking for 1 minute, until the second side is golden. Use the spoon to remove the doughnuts from the pot and put them on a cooling rack to drain. Repeat this process with the remaining doughnuts, being careful to maintain the oil heat at about 350 degrees F.

To make the glaze, put the confectioners' sugar in a medium bowl. Add the coconut milk, mixing until smooth. For a vanilla glaze, stir in the vanilla extract. Alternatively, for a hint of orange flavor, stir in the orange zest.

Dip the doughnuts into the glaze, being careful not to burn your fingers. Let cool for 5 minutes. Serve warm.

**TIP:** If you love the taste of nutmeg, increase the amount to 2 teaspoons.

**Cinnamon-Sugar Doughnuts:** Fry as directed. Omit the glaze. Put 1½ cups of confectioners' sugar, sifted, in a shallow bowl. Stir in 1 tablespoon of ground cinnamon until well combined. Coat each doughnut with the mixture after frying.

Per large doughnut: calories: 382, protein: 3 g, fat: 19 g, carbohydrate: 50 g, dietary fiber: 3 g, sodium: 154 mg

These baked treats taste best when made with peaches **picked fresh** at the height of their season. The fritters don't become crispy on the outside like deep-fried ones. Rather, they are **tender and light,** without all the added fat.

# BAKED PEACH Fritters WITH LEMON GLAZE

FREE OF: LEGUMES, NIGHTSHADES, NUTS, PEANUTS, SEEDS, SOY                    YIELD: ABOUT 18 FRITTERS

## FRITTERS

⅔ cup warm water

2½ teaspoons active dry yeast

½ teaspoon unrefined cane sugar

¼ cup agave nectar

¼ cup warm plain or vanilla nondairy milk

3 tablespoons coconut oil, at room temperature

1 teaspoon vanilla extract

1 teaspoon cider vinegar

¾ cup sorghum flour

½ cup arrowroot starch

½ cup millet flour

¼ cup sweet rice flour, plus more as needed

2½ teaspoons baking powder

2¼ teaspoons xanthan gum

2 teaspoons ground cinnamon

1 teaspoon ground nutmeg

½ teaspoon sea salt

2 ripe peaches, chopped (about 1½ cups)

## GLAZE

¾ cup confectioners' sugar, sifted

2 tablespoons freshly squeezed lemon juice

½ teaspoon vanilla extract

Line a baking sheet with parchment paper.

To make the fritters, put the water in a large measuring cup. Stir in the yeast and sugar. Let stand for about 5 minutes, until the yeast has bubbled and foamed about ½ inch.

Put the agave nectar, nondairy milk, oil, vanilla extract, and vinegar in a heavy-duty stand mixer or a large bowl. Using the stand mixer or a hand mixer, beat on medium speed until the ingredients are well combined.

Put the sorghum flour, arrowroot starch, millet flour, ¼ cup of the sweet rice flour, baking powder, xanthan gum, cinnamon, nutmeg, and salt in a medium bowl. Stir with a dry whisk until combined.

Turn the mixer to low speed and gradually add the proofed yeast mixture and the flour mixture to the agave nectar mixture to make a dough. Turn off the mixer and scrape down the sides of the bowl with a rubber spatula. Resume mixing on medium-high speed for 3 minutes. Reduce the speed to low. Add the peaches and mix just until they are evenly distributed. If the peaches are very ripe and juicy, add 1 to 2 additional tablespoons of sweet rice flour. The consistency should be thick, soft, and slightly moist—but not wet.

To form the fritters, use a cookie scoop or a spoon to drop heaping tablespoons of the mixture onto the lined baking sheet, leaving about 1½ inches between the fritters. Smooth with your fingertips. Let rise uncovered in a warm, draft-free place for about 40 minutes, until doubled in size.

About 10 minutes before the dough is done rising, preheat the oven to 350 degrees F. (If the dough is rising in the oven, be sure to remove it first.)

Bake for 18 to 22 minutes, until lightly browned on the bottom. Immediately transfer the fritters to a cooling rack. Let them cool while you prepare the glaze.

To make the glaze, put the confectioners' sugar in a small bowl. Stir in the lemon juice and vanilla extract until well combined. Stir in just enough water to thin the glaze if necessary. Drizzle over the fritters. Serve warm.

Per fritter: calories: 114, protein: 2 g, fat: 3 g, carbohydrate: 21 g, dietary fiber: 2 g, sodium: 112 mg

A twist on traditional focaccia, this chewy flatbread features **sweet dates** and **crunchy walnuts.** For a savory version, see Sun-Dried Tomato Focaccia with Shallots and Herbs (page 119).

# DATE AND WALNUT *Focaccia*

FREE OF: LEGUMES, NIGHTSHADES, PEANUTS, SEEDS, SOY                    YIELD: 8 TO 10 SERVINGS

**1 cup plus 1 tablespoon warm water**
**1 tablespoon active dry yeast**
**1 teaspoon unrefined cane sugar**
**1 cup sorghum flour**
**½ cup quinoa flour**
**¼ cup arrowroot starch**
**¼ cup tapioca flour**
**2 teaspoons xanthan gum**
**1 teaspoon ground nutmeg**
**¾ teaspoon sea salt**
**2 tablespoons agave nectar**
**1 tablespoon canola oil or nut oil**
**1 teaspoon vanilla extract**
**1 teaspoon cider vinegar**
**⅓ cup chopped soft dates**
**⅓ cup coarsely chopped walnuts**
**Confectioners' sugar, for serving**

Line a 9 x 13-inch baking pan with parchment paper. Generously oil the parchment paper.

Put the water in a large measuring cup. Stir in the yeast and sugar. Let stand for about 5 minutes, until the yeast has bubbled and foamed about ½ inch.

Put the sorghum flour, quinoa flour, arrowroot starch, tapioca flour, xanthan gum, nutmeg, and salt in a heavy-duty stand mixer or a large bowl. Stir with a dry whisk until combined.

Add the agave nectar, oil, vanilla extract, and vinegar to the yeast mixture. Turn the stand mixer or a hand mixer on low speed and gradually add the yeast mixture to the flour mixture to make a dough. Turn off the mixer and scrape down the sides of the bowl with a rubber spatula. Resume mixing on medium-high speed for 4 minutes. The dough will be very sticky, similar to thick muffin batter. Stir in the dates and walnuts until evenly distributed.

Use the spatula to scrape the dough onto the lined pan. With oiled hands, spread the dough until it is about ¼-inch thick. Do not smooth; the top should remain bumpy (this will give it a rustic appearance). Let rise uncovered in a warm, draft-free place for about 40 minutes, until doubled in size.

About 10 minutes before the dough is done rising, preheat the oven to 400 degrees F. (If the dough is rising in the oven, be sure to remove it first.)

Use your fingers to gently indent the top of the dough. Bake for 30 to 35 minutes, until golden brown. Generously sprinkle confectioners' sugar over the focaccia while it is still hot. Carefully remove the focaccia from the pan and put it on a cooling rack. Let cool for at least 10 minutes before serving.

**VARIATION:** Add 1 tablespoon of finely chopped fresh rosemary to the flour mixture.

Per serving: calories: 182, protein: 4 g, fat: 5 g, carbohydrate: 30 g, dietary fiber: 4 g, sodium: 179 mg

Here, the dough is topped with apples, cardamom, cinnamon, and raisins, then folded over so these ingredients become a **flavorful filling.** Topped with a sweet vanilla glaze, this **breakfast cake** is in a class by itself.

# FREE-FORM Apple Spice Cake WITH VANILLA GLAZE

FREE OF: LEGUMES, NIGHTSHADES, NUTS, PEANUTS, SOY                    YIELD: 8 TO 10 SERVINGS

## CAKE

½ cup warm plain or vanilla nondairy milk

2¼ teaspoons active dry yeast

1 tablespoon ground flaxseeds

1 tablespoon unrefined cane sugar

¾ cup millet flour

½ cup arrowroot starch

½ cup sorghum flour

⅓ cup quinoa flour

¼ cup tapioca flour

1½ teaspoons xanthan gum

½ teaspoon sea salt

¼ cup unsweetened applesauce

¼ cup warm water

2 tablespoons agave nectar

2 tablespoons coconut oil, melted

## FILLING

**2 tart apples** (such as granny smith), **cored and thinly sliced** (about 2 cups)

⅔ cup unrefined cane sugar

1 teaspoon ground cardamom

1 teaspoon ground cinnamon

⅓ cup raisins

To make the cake, pour the nondairy milk into a large measuring cup. Stir in the yeast, flaxseeds, and sugar. Let stand for about 5 minutes, until the yeast has bubbled and foamed about ½ inch.

Put the millet flour, arrowroot starch, sorghum flour, quinoa flour, tapioca flour, xanthan gum, and salt in a heavy-duty stand mixer or a large bowl. Stir with a dry whisk until combined.

Put the applesauce, water, agave nectar, and oil in a small bowl. Stir until well combined. Turn the stand mixer or a hand mixer on low speed and gradually add the proofed yeast mixture to make a dough. Turn off the mixer and scrape down the sides of the bowl with a rubber spatula. Resume mixing on medium-high speed for 2 minutes. The dough will be very sticky, similar to a thick muffin batter.

To make the filling, put the sliced apples, sugar, cardamom, and cinnamon in a small bowl. Toss until the apples are coated with the sugar and spices.

Line a baking sheet with a piece of parchment paper (20 to 22 inches long). Lightly oil the parchment paper. Use the spatula to scrape the dough onto the parchment paper. Top with a second piece of oiled parchment paper about the same size, with the oiled side facing the dough. Use a rolling pin to roll the dough between the pieces of parchment paper to form an 18 x 15-inch rectangle, about ¼-inch thick. Spread the filling over the center of the dough, leaving a 3-inch border on each side and a 2-inch border on the top and bottom. Sprinkle the raisins over the filling.

Per serving: calories: 295, protein: 4 g, fat: 5 g, carbohydrate: 62 g, dietary fiber: 4 g, sodium: 246 mg

## GLAZE

¾ cup confectioners' sugar, sifted

1 tablespoon plain or vanilla nondairy milk, plus more if needed

1 teaspoon vanilla extract

Use the spatula to fold the dough around the apple mixture, leaving about 2 inches of the center exposed. Because the dough will be sticky, it may be difficult to fold it all at once, so fold a section at a time. Let rise uncovered in a warm, draft-free place for about 40 minutes, until doubled in size.

About 10 minutes before the dough is done rising, preheat the oven to 375 degrees F. (If the dough is rising in the oven, be sure to remove it first.)

Bake for 20 to 25 minutes, until the cake is lightly browned and the apples have softened. Use the parchment paper to help transfer the cake to a cooling rack to cool.

To make the glaze, put the confectioners' sugar, non-dairy milk, and vanilla extract in a small bowl. Stir until well combined. Stir in just enough additional nondairy milk to thin the glaze if necessary. Drizzle over the warm cake. Slide the cake off the parchment paper and onto a large serving dish. Serve warm.

# Savory Yeast Breads

*Good bread is the most fundamentally satisfying of all foods.*

JAMES BEARD, *AMERICAN CHEF*

See Wholesome Flax Bread, page 99.

I received an overwhelming amount of positive feedback after posting this recipe on a popular food website. Nutritious and delicious, Wholesome Flax Bread is the ultimate sandwich bread. Feel free to experiment with different flour combinations here.

# Wholesome FLAX BREAD

FREE OF: NIGHTSHADES,* NUTS, PEANUTS, SOY                                        YIELD: 12 TO 18 SLICES

1½ cups plus 1 tablespoon warm water

2 tablespoons pure maple syrup or agave nectar

2½ teaspoons active dry yeast

¼ cup plus 3 tablespoons ground flaxseeds

¾ cup plus 2 tablespoons sorghum flour

½ cup arrowroot starch or potato starch (*for nightshade-free, use arrowroot starch)

½ cup quinoa flour

¼ cup garfava or bean flour

¼ cup tapioca flour

2½ teaspoons xanthan gum

1 teaspoon sea salt

2 tablespoons canola oil

2 teaspoons cider vinegar

Lightly oil an 8½ x 4½-inch loaf pan.

Put 1 cup of the water in a large measuring cup. Stir in the maple syrup and yeast. Let stand for about 5 minutes, until the yeast has bubbled and foamed about ½ inch.

Put the remaining ½ cup plus 1 tablespoon of water in a heavy-duty stand mixer or a large bowl. Stir in 3 tablespoons of the flaxseeds. Let stand until thickened, about 5 minutes.

Put the remaining ¼ cup of flaxseeds, the sorghum flour, arrowroot starch, quinoa flour, garfava flour, tapioca flour, xanthan gum, and salt in a medium bowl. Stir with a dry whisk until combined.

Add the oil and vinegar to the thickened flaxseed mixture. Using the stand mixer or a hand mixer, beat on medium speed for about 30 seconds, until well combined. Turn the mixer to low speed and gradually add the proofed yeast mixture and the flour mixture to make a dough. Turn off the mixer and scrape down the sides of the bowl with a rubber spatula. Resume mixing on medium-high speed for 5 minutes. The dough will be very sticky, similar to thick muffin batter.

Scrape the dough into the prepared pan using a rubber spatula. Smooth out the top. Let rise uncovered in a warm, draft-free place for about 70 minutes, just until the dough reaches the top of the pan.

About 10 minutes before the dough is done rising, preheat the oven to 350 degrees F. (If the dough is rising in the oven, be sure to remove it first.)

Bake for 40 to 45 minutes, until the top of the loaf is browned and a toothpick inserted in the center of the loaf comes out clean. Carefully remove the loaf from the pan and put it on a cooling rack. Let cool completely before slicing.

Per slice: calories: 117, protein: 3 g, fat: 4 g, carbohydrate: 18 g, dietary fiber: 3 g, sodium: 145 mg

Inspired by my favorite mole poblano, this bread features two key ingredients found in the popular Mexican sauce: chili powder and cocoa powder.

# MEXICAN Mole BREAD

FREE OF: LEGUMES, NUTS, PEANUTS, SOY                    YIELD: 10 TO 12 SLICES

1¼ cups plus 6 tablespoons warm water

2½ teaspoons active dry yeast

3 teaspoons unrefined cane sugar

2 tablespoons ground flaxseeds

1¼ cups sorghum flour

½ cup teff flour

¼ cup arrowroot starch or potato starch

¼ cup tapioca flour

1 tablespoon unsweetened cocoa powder, sifted

2½ teaspoons xanthan gum

1¾ teaspoons chili powder

¾ teaspoon ground cinnamon

½ teaspoon sea salt

¼ teaspoon cayenne

2 tablespoons light molasses

2 tablespoons canola oil

1 teaspoon cider vinegar

Lightly oil an 8½ x 4½-inch loaf pan.

Put 1¼ cups of the water in a large measuring cup. Stir in the yeast and 1 teaspoon of the sugar. Let stand for about 5 minutes, until the yeast has bubbled and foamed about ½ inch.

Put the remaining 6 tablespoons of water in a heavy-duty stand mixer or a large bowl. Stir in the flaxseeds. Let stand until thickened, about 5 minutes.

Put the sorghum flour, teff flour, arrowroot starch, tapioca flour, cocoa powder, xanthan gum, chili powder, cinnamon, salt, cayenne, and remaining 2 teaspoons of sugar in a medium bowl. Stir with a dry whisk until combined.

Add the molasses, oil, and vinegar to the thickened flaxseed mixture. Using the stand mixer or a hand mixer, beat on medium speed for about 1 minute until well combined. Turn the mixer to low speed and gradually add the proofed yeast mixture and the flour mixture to make a dough. Turn off the mixer and scrape down the sides of the bowl with a rubber spatula. Resume mixing on medium-high speed for 5 minutes. The dough will be very sticky, similar to thick muffin batter.

Scrape the dough into the prepared pan using a rubber spatula. Smooth out the top. Let rise uncovered in a warm, draft-free place for about 70 minutes, just until the dough reaches the top of the pan.

About 10 minutes before the dough is done rising, preheat the oven to 350 degrees F. (If the dough is rising in the oven, be sure to remove it first.)

Bake for 40 to 45 minutes, until the top of the loaf is browned and a toothpick inserted in the center of the loaf comes out clean. Carefully remove the loaf from the pan and put it on a cooling rack. Let cool completely before slicing.

Per slice: calories: 150, protein: 3 g, fat: 4 g, carbohydrate: 26 g, dietary fiber: 4 g, sodium: 102 mg

This **hearty loaf** is brimming with a multitude of grains. Toasted hempseeds add a savory **nutty flavor** and crunch.

# Multigrain HEMPSEED BREAD

FREE OF: LEGUMES, NIGHTSHADES, NUTS, PEANUTS, SOY                    YIELD: 10 TO 12 SLICES

1½ cups plus 2 tablespoons warm water

3 tablespoons plus 1 teaspoon unrefined cane sugar

1 scant tablespoon active dry yeast

¾ cup sorghum flour

½ cup millet flour

½ cup quinoa flour

½ cup tapioca flour

½ cup teff flour

¼ cup arrowroot starch

2 tablespoons sweet rice flour

2 teaspoons xanthan gum

1 teaspoon sea salt

⅓ cup plus 2 tablespoons hempseeds, toasted (see page 20)

3 teaspoons canola oil

1 teaspoon cider vinegar

Lightly oil a 9 x 5-inch loaf pan.

Put the water in a large measuring cup. Stir in 1 teaspoon of the sugar and the yeast. Let stand for about 5 minutes, until the yeast has bubbled and foamed about ½ inch.

Put the sorghum flour, millet flour, quinoa flour, tapioca flour, teff flour, arrowroot starch, sweet rice flour, xanthan gum, salt, and remaining 3 tablespoons of sugar in a heavy-duty stand mixer or a large bowl. Stir with a dry whisk until combined. Stir in ⅓ cup of the hempseeds.

Turn the stand mixer or a hand mixer on low speed and gradually add the proofed yeast mixture, 2 teaspoons of the oil, and the vinegar to the flour mixture to make a dough. Turn off the mixer and scrape down the sides of the bowl with a rubber spatula. Resume mixing on medium-high speed for 4 minutes. The dough will be very sticky, similar to thick muffin batter.

Scrape the dough into the prepared pan using a rubber spatula. Smooth out the top. Let rise uncovered in a warm, draft-free place for about 70 minutes, just until the dough reaches the top of the pan.

About 10 minutes before the dough is done rising, preheat the oven to 350 degrees F. (If the dough is rising in the oven, be sure to remove it first.)

Brush the top of the dough with the remaining teaspoon of oil. Sprinkle with the remaining 2 tablespoons of hempseeds.

Bake for 50 to 60 minutes, until the top of the loaf is browned and a toothpick inserted in the center of the loaf comes out clean. Carefully remove the loaf from the pan and put it on a cooling rack. Let cool completely before slicing.

**TIP:** If you prefer a more nutty flavor and texture, increase the amount of hempseeds to ½ cup.

Per slice: calories: 178, protein: 5 g, fat: 3 g, carbohydrate: 33 g, dietary fiber: 3 g, sodium: 197 mg

This classic bread has a *crusty exterior* and a soft interior. It's the ideal base for bruschetta; garlic bread; or a sandwich filled with grilled garden vegetables, baby spinach, and hummus.

# Rustic FRENCH BREAD

FREE OF: NIGHTSHADES, NUTS, PEANUTS

YIELD: 15 TO 20 SLICES

¾ cup plus 2 tablespoons warm water

1 tablespoon ground flaxseeds

3 teaspoons unrefined cane sugar

1 tablespoon active dry yeast

¾ cup sorghum flour

¼ cup arrowroot starch

¼ cup tapioca flour

¼ cup teff flour

1½ teaspoons xanthan gum

½ teaspoon sea salt

1 tablespoon vegan buttery spread, melted and cooled, or olive oil

½ teaspoon cider vinegar

Lightly oil a baking sheet or line it with parchment paper.

Put the water in a large measuring cup. Stir in the flaxseeds, 1 teaspoon of the sugar, and the yeast. Let stand for about 5 minutes, until the yeast has bubbled and foamed about ½ inch.

Put the sorghum flour, arrowroot starch, tapioca flour, teff flour, xanthan gum, salt, and remaining 2 teaspoons of sugar in a heavy-duty stand mixer or a large bowl. Stir with a dry whisk until combined.

Turn the stand mixer or a hand mixer on low speed. Gradually add the proofed yeast mixture, vegan buttery spread, and vinegar to the flour mixture to make a dough. Turn off the mixer and scrape down the sides of the bowl with a rubber spatula. Resume mixing on medium-high speed for 4 minutes. The dough will be very sticky, similar to thick muffin batter.

Use the spatula to scrape the dough onto the prepared baking sheet. With oiled hands, form a long, thin loaf. Let rise uncovered in a warm, draft-free place for 35 to 45 minutes, until doubled in size.

About 10 minutes before the dough is done rising, preheat the oven to 400 degrees F. (If the dough is rising in the oven, be sure to remove it first.)

Use a sharp, serrated knife to make three to four slits in the top of the loaf. Bake for 30 to 40 minutes, until the top of the loaf is browned and a toothpick inserted in the center of the loaf comes out clean. Carefully remove the loaf from the pan and put it on a cooling rack. Let cool completely before slicing.

Per slice: calories: 55, protein: 1 g, fat: 1 g, carbohydrate: 10 g, dietary fiber: 1 g, sodium: 131 mg

Pumpernickel is a type of **wholesome**, slightly sweet rye bread with an **earthy** taste. This gluten-free version uses caraway seeds, cocoa powder, and molasses to produce a similar taste, without a speck of rye.

# soft Pumpernickel BREADSTICKS

FREE OF: LEGUMES, NIGHTSHADES,* NUTS, PEANUTS, SOY                    YIELD: TWELVE 6-INCH BREADSTICKS

½ cup plus 2 tablespoons warm water

2 teaspoons active dry yeast

1 teaspoon unrefined cane sugar

⅓ cup sorghum flour

¼ cup teff flour

3 tablespoons potato starch or arrowroot starch (*for nightshade-free, use arrowroot starch)

3 tablespoons tapioca flour

3 teaspoons caraway seeds

1 tablespoon unsweetened cocoa powder, sifted

1¼ teaspoons xanthan gum

½ teaspoon sea salt, plus more as needed

1 tablespoon light molasses

1 tablespoon canola oil or extra-virgin olive oil, plus more for brushing the dough

1 teaspoon cider vinegar

Per breadstick: calories: 63, protein: 2 g, fat: 2 g, carbohydrate: 11 g, dietary fiber: 2 g, sodium: 92 mg

Line a baking sheet with parchment paper.

Put the water in a large measuring cup. Stir in the yeast and sugar. Let stand for about 5 minutes, until the yeast has bubbled and foamed about ½ inch.

Put the sorghum flour, teff flour, potato starch, tapioca flour, 2 teaspoons of the caraway seeds, cocoa powder, xanthan gum, and salt in a heavy-duty stand mixer or a large bowl. Stir with a dry whisk until combined.

Add the molasses, oil, and vinegar to the proofed yeast mixture. Turn the stand mixer or a hand mixer on low speed. Gradually add the yeast mixture to the flour mixture to make a dough. Turn off the mixer and scrape down the sides of the bowl with a rubber spatula. Resume mixing on medium-high speed for 4 minutes. The dough will be very sticky, similar to thick muffin batter.

Lightly oil the inside of a large ziplock bag. Use scissors to snip off ½ to ¾ inches from the bottom corner of the bag. Alternatively, use a pastry bag with a ½- to ¾-inch tip.

Use the spatula to scrape the dough into the bag, and then seal the bag closed. Gently squeeze the bag and pipe the dough into strips, about 5 inches long, onto the lined baking sheet. Leave about 1 inch between the breadsticks. Let rise uncovered in a warm, draft-free place for 20 to 30 minutes, until doubled in size.

About 10 minutes before the dough is done rising, preheat the oven to 425 degrees F. (If the dough is rising in the oven, be sure to remove it first.)

Brush the dough lightly with oil. Sprinkle with the remaining teaspoon of caraway seeds and lightly sprinkle with salt.

Bake for 10 to 12 minutes, until firm to the touch and lightly browned. Carefully remove the breadsticks from the pan and put them in a serving dish. Let cool for 5 minutes. Serve warm.

Simple to prepare, these savory breadsticks are perfect for dunking in your favorite marinara sauce.

# ITALIAN Breadsticks

FREE OF: LEGUMES, NIGHTSHADES,* NUTS, PEANUTS, SEEDS, SOY          YIELD: TWELVE 6-INCH BREADSTICKS

½ cup plus 2 tablespoons warm water

2 teaspoons active dry yeast

1 teaspoon unrefined cane sugar

⅓ cup sorghum flour

¼ cup quinoa flour

¼ cup tapioca flour

3 tablespoons potato starch or arrowroot starch (*for nightshade-free, use arrowroot starch)

1¼ teaspoons xanthan gum

1 teaspoon italian seasoning

½ teaspoon sea salt, plus more as needed

¼ teaspoon garlic powder

1 tablespoon agave nectar

1 tablespoon canola oil or extra-virgin olive oil, plus more for brushing the dough

1 teaspoon cider vinegar

Per breadstick: calories: 60, protein: 1 g, fat: 1 g, carbohydrate: 11 g, dietary fiber: 1 g, sodium: 91 mg

Line a baking sheet with parchment paper.

Put the water in a large measuring cup. Stir in the yeast and sugar. Let stand for about 5 minutes, until the yeast has bubbled and foamed about ½ inch.

Put the sorghum flour, quinoa flour, tapioca flour, potato starch, xanthan gum, italian seasoning, salt, and garlic powder in a heavy-duty stand mixer or a large bowl. Stir with a dry whisk until combined.

Add the agave nectar, oil, and vinegar to the proofed yeast mixture. Turn the stand mixer or a hand mixer on low speed. Gradually add the yeast mixture to the flour mixture to make a dough. Turn off the mixer and scrape down the sides of the bowl with a rubber spatula. Resume mixing on medium-high speed for 4 minutes. The dough will be very sticky, similar to thick muffin batter.

Lightly oil the inside of a large ziplock bag. Use scissors to snip off ½ to ¾ inches from the bottom corner of the bag. Alternatively, use a pastry bag with a ½- to ¾-inch tip.

Use the spatula to scrape the dough into the bag, and then seal the bag closed. Gently squeeze the bag and pipe the dough into strips, about 5 inches long, onto the lined baking sheet. Leave about 1 inch between the breadsticks. Let rise uncovered in a warm, draft-free place for 20 to 30 minutes, until doubled in size.

About 10 minutes before the dough is done rising, preheat the oven to 425 degrees F. (If the dough is rising in the oven, be sure to remove it first.)

Brush the dough lightly with oil. Bake for 10 to 12 minutes, until firm to the touch and lightly browned. Carefully remove the breadsticks from the pan and put them in a serving dish. Let cool for 5 minutes. Serve warm.

Airy and light, these english muffins taste just like their wheat-filled counterparts. The similarities don't stop there: these muffins also can be split in half without the aid of a knife. Serve toasted with homemade preserves and a smear of vegan buttery spread.

# Easy ENGLISH MUFFINS

FREE OF: NIGHTSHADES, NUTS, PEANUTS

YIELD: 6 ENGLISH MUFFINS

Whole-grain cornmeal, for the pan

¾ cup warm water

1 tablespoon plus 1 teaspoon agave nectar

2½ teaspoons active dry yeast

2 teaspoons ground flaxseeds

½ cup quinoa flour

½ cup sorghum flour

¼ cup arrowroot starch

¼ cup tapioca flour

1 teaspoon xanthan gum

½ teaspoon sea salt

1½ tablespoons vegan buttery spread, melted

½ teaspoon cider vinegar

Line a baking sheet with parchment paper. Sprinkle lightly with cornmeal. Lightly oil six english muffin rings and put them on the lined baking sheet. Alternatively, form six 4-inch rings out of aluminum foil. Oil each ring, then place them on the baking sheet.

Put the water in a large measuring cup. Stir in 1 teaspoon of the agave nectar, the yeast, and flaxseeds. Let stand for about 5 minutes, until the yeast has bubbled and foamed about ½ inch.

Put the quinoa flour, sorghum flour, arrowroot starch, tapioca flour, xanthan gum, and salt in a heavy-duty mixer or a large bowl. Stir with a dry whisk until combined.

Add the remaining tablespoon of agave nectar, ½ teaspoon of the vegan buttery spread, and the vinegar to the proofed yeast mixture. Turn the stand mixer or a hand mixer on low speed and gradually add the yeast mixture to the flour mixture to make a dough. Turn off the mixer and scrape down the sides of the bowl with a rubber spatula. Resume mixing on medium-high speed for 2 minutes. The dough will be very sticky, similar to thick muffin batter.

Spoon the dough into the prepared rings. Dip your fingertips into the remaining vegan buttery spread and smooth the tops evenly, pressing the dough to the edges of the rings. (This is a key step; otherwise the english muffins will rise like buns.) Let rise uncovered in a warm, draft-free place for 40 to 60 minutes, until doubled in size.

About 10 minutes before the dough is done rising, preheat the oven to 375 degrees F. (If the dough is rising in the oven, be sure to remove it first.)

Bake for 13 to 15 minutes, until the edges are firm but not yet browned. Carefully remove the english muffins from the rings and put them on a cooling rack. Let cool for at least 15 minutes. Split with a fork. Serve warm.

**Cinnamon-Raisin English Muffins:** Replace the agave nectar with pure maple syrup. Add ⅓ cup of raisins and ¾ teaspoon of ground cinnamon to the flour mixture.

Per muffin: calories: 157, protein: 3 g, fat: 3 g, carbohydrate: 28 g, dietary fiber: 3 g, sodium: 201 mg

The two most **popular bagel** varieties hail from Montreal and New York. Montreal bagels contain no added salt, are boiled in honey-sweetened water, and are baked in a wood-fired oven. New York bagels contain salt, are boiled in unsweetened water, and are baked in a standard oven. **Chewy** on the outside and **tender** on the inside, these bagels take cues from the New York version.

# New York-STYLE BAGELS

FREE OF: LEGUMES,* NIGHTSHADES,* NUTS, PEANUTS, SOY

YIELD: 8 BAGELS

Whole-grain cornmeal, for the pans

⅔ cup unsweetened nondairy milk, plus more for brushing the dough

6 tablespoons warm water

3 tablespoons agave nectar

2 tablespoons active dry yeast

1 tablespoon ground flaxseeds

1 cup sorghum flour

½ cup amaranth, quinoa, bean, or millet flour (*for legume-free, use amaranth, quinoa, or millet flour)

½ cup arrowroot starch or potato starch (*for nightshade-free, use arrowroot starch)

½ cup tapioca flour, plus more for handling the dough

1 tablespoon baking powder

2 teaspoons xanthan gum

½ teaspoon baking soda

1 teaspoon sea salt

½ teaspoon cider vinegar

Hempseeds (optional)

Poppy seeds (optional)

Sesame seeds (optional)

Line a baking sheet with parchment paper. Sprinkle lightly with cornmeal. Fill a dutch oven or a large saucepan with salted water.

Put the nondairy milk and water in a large measuring cup. Stir in 1 tablespoon of the agave nectar, the yeast, and flaxseeds. Let stand for about 5 minutes, until the yeast has bubbled and foamed about ½ inch.

Put the sorghum flour, amaranth flour, arrowroot starch, tapioca flour, baking powder, xanthan gum, baking soda, and salt in a heavy-duty stand mixer or a large bowl. Stir with a dry whisk until combined.

Turn the stand mixer or a held-held mixer on low speed and add the proofed yeast mixture, vinegar, and remaining 2 tablespoons of agave nectar to make a dough. Turn off the mixer and scrape down the sides of the bowl with a rubber spatula. Resume mixing on medium-high speed for 5 minutes.

Use the spatula to scrape the dough onto a clean, lightly floured work surface. With oiled hands, shape the dough into a large ball. If it is too sticky to handle, sprinkle the dough and work surface very lightly with tapioca flour. Divide the dough into 8 equal portions, forming each into a puffy pancake shape, about 4 inches in diameter. Use your thumb to create a hole in the center of each to form the bagels. Put the bagels on the lined baking sheet. Let rise uncovered in a warm, draft-free place for about 55 minutes, until doubled in size.

About 10 minutes before the dough is done rising, preheat the oven to 375 degrees F. (If the dough is rising in the oven, be sure to remove it first.)

Per bagel: calories: 192, protein: 5 g, fat: 2 g, carbohydrate: 40 g, dietary fiber: 4 g, sodium: 494 mg

Bring the salted water to a boil. Use a slotted spoon to gently put the unbaked bagels in the water, a few at a time. Let boil for 20 seconds per side. Transfer to the lined baking sheet. Repeat until all are boiled.

Brush each bagel with nondairy milk. Sprinkle with hemp-seeds, poppy seeds, or sesame seeds if using.

Bake for 15 to 18 minutes, until lightly browned. Carefully transfer the bagels to a cooling rack. Let cool for at least 20 minutes before slicing.

**TIP:** Boiling the bagels creates their signature chewy outer crust. Because this crust becomes even chewier when a frozen bagel is defrosted in the microwave, I recommend heating frozen bagels on low heat in the oven until warmed through. Alternatively, slice them in half and toast them.

These buns are the **ideal complement** to your favorite veggie burger and fixings, such as my favorite combo: crisp lettuce, yellow mustard, caramelized onions, tangy pickles, and juicy tomatoes.

# Burger BUNS

FREE OF: LEGUMES, NIGHTSHADES, PEANUTS, SOY                                    YIELD: 6 BUNS

1¾ cups warm water

2 tablespoons plus 1 teaspoon agave nectar

2½ teaspoons active dry yeast

3 tablespoons ground flaxseeds

1¼ cups sorghum flour

⅔ cup arrowroot starch

½ cup quinoa flour

⅓ cup tapioca flour, plus more for handling the dough

2 tablespoons finely ground almonds

2½ teaspoons xanthan gum

1½ teaspoons sea salt

2 tablespoons extra-virgin olive oil

1 teaspoon cider vinegar

Line a baking sheet with parchment paper. Lightly oil six english muffin rings and put them on the lined baking sheet. Alternatively, form six 4-inch rings out of aluminum foil. Oil each ring, then place them on the baking sheet.

Put 1 cup of the water in a large measuring cup. Stir in 1 teaspoon of the agave nectar and the yeast. Let stand for about 5 minutes, until the yeast has bubbled and foamed about ½ inch.

Put the remaining ¾ cup of water in a heavy-duty stand mixer or a large bowl. Stir in the flaxseeds. Let stand until thickened, about 5 minutes.

Put the sorghum flour, arrowroot starch, quinoa flour, tapioca flour, almonds, xanthan gum, and salt in a medium bowl. Stir with a dry whisk until combined.

Add the remaining 2 tablespoons of agave nectar, the oil, and vinegar to the thickened flaxseed mixture. Using the stand mixer or a hand mixer, beat on medium speed until well mixed. Turn the mixer to low speed and gradually add the proofed yeast mixture and flour mixture to make a dough. Turn off the mixer and scrape down the sides of the bowl with a rubber spatula. Resume mixing on medium-high speed for 4 minutes. The dough will be very sticky, similar to thick muffin batter.

Use the spatula to divide the dough into 6 equal portions and transfer them to the prepared rings. Use oiled hands to form the dough into smooth, round buns. Leave about 1 inch between the buns. Let rise uncovered in a warm, draft-free place for about 60 minutes, until doubled in size.

Per bun: calories: 316, protein: 6 g, fat: 9 g, carbohydrate: 54 g, dietary fiber: 7 g, sodium: 537 mg

About 10 minutes before the dough is done rising, preheat the oven to 350 degrees F. (If the dough is rising in the oven, be sure to remove it first.)

Bake for 15 to 20 minutes, until lightly browned. Carefully remove the buns from the rings and put them on a cooling rack. Let cool for at least 20 minutes before slicing.

**Veggie Dog or Submarine Sandwich Buns:** Use a rubber spatula to scrape the dough into a well-oiled, large ziplock bag and seal the bag closed. Use scissors to snip off about 1¼ inches from the bottom corner of the bag. Alternatively, use a pastry bag with a 1¼-inch tip. Gently squeeze the bag and pipe the dough into strips, about 4 inches long, onto the lined pan. Leave about 1 inch between the buns. Let rise and bake as directed.

This **sandwich roll** has just the right texture—crusty outside and fluffy inside. Dijon mustard, thyme, and pure maple syrup add just the right amount of flavor, without overpowering the sandwich fillings.

# Crusty ROLLS WITH DIJON AND THYME

FREE OF: LEGUMES, NIGHTSHADES,* PEANUTS, SOY               YIELD: 6 ROLLS

½ cup warm water

3 tablespoons pure maple syrup

2½ teaspoons active dry yeast

1⅛ cups warmed club soda (see tip)

3 tablespoons ground flaxseeds

1¼ cups sorghum flour

⅔ cup potato starch or arrowroot starch (*for nightshade-free, use arrowroot starch)

½ cup quinoa flour

⅓ cup tapioca flour, plus more for handling the dough

¼ cup finely ground almonds

1 tablespoon dried thyme

2½ teaspoons xanthan gum

1½ teaspoons sea salt

2 tablespoons dijon mustard

2 tablespoons extra-virgin olive oil

1 teaspoon cider vinegar

2 tablespoons unsweetened nondairy milk

Per roll: calories: 365, protein: 8 g, fat: 11 g, carbohydrate: 58 g, dietary fiber: 7 g, sodium: 692 mg

Line a baking sheet with parchment paper. Lightly oil six english muffin rings and put them on the lined baking sheet. Alternatively, use aluminum foil to form six 4-inch rings. Oil each ring, then place them on the baking sheet. Or lightly oil a bun pan or a muffin-top pan.

Put the water in a large measuring cup. Stir in 1 tablespoon of the maple syrup and the yeast. Let stand for about 5 minutes, until the yeast has bubbled and foamed about ½ inch.

Pour the club soda into a heavy-duty stand mixer or a large bowl. Stir in the flaxseeds. Let stand until thickened, about 5 minutes.

Put the sorghum flour, potato starch, quinoa flour, tapioca flour, almonds, thyme, xanthan gum, and salt in a medium bowl. Stir with a dry whisk until combined.

Add the remaining 2 tablespoons of maple syrup, the mustard, oil, and vinegar to the thickened flaxseed mixture. Using the stand mixer or a hand mixer, beat on medium speed until well blended. Turn the mixer to low speed and gradually add the proofed yeast mixture and the flour mixture to make a dough. Turn off the mixer and scrape down the sides of the bowl with a rubber spatula. Resume mixing on medium-high speed for 4 minutes. The dough will be very sticky, similar to thick muffin batter.

Divide the dough into 6 equal portions and use the spatula to put them in the prepared rings or pan. Use oiled hands to form the dough into smooth rounds. Let rise uncovered in a warm, draft-free place for about 60 minutes, until doubled in size.

About 10 minutes before the dough is done rising, preheat the oven to 350 degrees F. (If the dough is rising in the oven, be sure to remove it first.)

Brush the dough with the nondairy milk. Bake for 15 to 20 minutes, until lightly browned. Carefully remove the rolls from the rings and put them on a cooling rack. Let cool for at least 20 minutes before slicing.

**TIP:** Club soda creates a fluffier rise, but water or nondairy milk will work as well. Simply substitute equal amounts of either warm water or nondairy milk for the club soda.

The **secret ingredient** in these tender rolls is avocado, which gives them a slightly crisp exterior and a buttery, fluffy interior with a hint of sweetness.

# SWEET Dinner ROLLS

FREE OF: LEGUMES, NIGHTSHADES, NUTS, PEANUTS, SEEDS, SOY                    YIELD: 10 TO 12 ROLLS

¼ cup warm water

1 tablespoon active dry yeast

1 teaspoon unrefined cane sugar

1½ small, ripe avocados, flesh removed and mashed (about ¾ cup)

¾ cup warm vegan buttermilk (see page 17)

2 tablespoons agave nectar

2 tablespoons canola oil

½ teaspoon sea salt

1 cup plus 3 tablespoons sorghum flour

¾ cup quinoa flour

½ cup arrowroot starch

½ cup tapioca flour

2½ teaspoons xanthan gum

1 teaspoon baking powder

Lightly oil a 12-cup muffin pan.

Put the water in a large measuring cup. Stir in the yeast and sugar. Let stand for about 5 minutes, until the yeast has bubbled and foamed about ½ inch.

Put the avocados, vegan buttermilk, agave nectar, oil, and salt in a heavy-duty stand mixer or a large bowl. Using the stand mixer or a hand mixer, beat on medium speed until well combined.

Put the sorghum flour, quinoa flour, arrowroot starch, tapioca flour, xanthan gum, and baking powder in a large bowl. Stir with a dry whisk until combined.

Turn the mixer to low speed and gradually add the proofed yeast mixture and the flour mixture to make a dough. Turn off the mixer and scrape down the sides of the bowl with a rubber spatula. Resume mixing on medium-high speed for 4 minutes. The dough will be very sticky.

To form cloverleaf rolls, use oiled hands to tear off small portions of the dough and roll them between your palms to make small balls, about the size of chestnuts. Put three balls in each muffin cup, pressing them together slightly. Repeat until all the dough has been used. Alternatively, roll a portion of dough between your palms to create a ball about 2 inches in diameter. Repeat until all the dough has been used. Put one ball in each muffin cup. Let rise uncovered in a warm, draft-free place for about 45 minutes, until doubled in size.

About 10 minutes before the dough is done rising, preheat the oven to 375 degrees F. (If the dough is rising in the oven, be sure to remove it first.)

Bake for 12 to 15 minutes, until golden brown. Let cool in the pan for 2 minutes. Carefully remove the rolls from the pan and put them in a serving dish. Let cool for 10 minutes. Serve warm.

Per roll: calories: 215, protein: 4 g, fat: 8 g, carbohydrate: 31 g, dietary fiber: 5 g, sodium: 141 mg

These **tender rolls,** which are covered with a **buttery and cheesy** coating, are made for dipping in a homemade marinara sauce. Adjust the amount of garlic to suit your taste.

# GARLICKY Pull-Apart ROLLS

FREE OF: NIGHTSHADES, NUTS, PEANUTS, SEEDS

YIELD: 10 TO 12 ROLLS

## ROLLS

1 cup warm water

4½ teaspoons unrefined cane sugar

1 tablespoon active dry yeast

¾ cup plus 2 tablespoons sorghum flour

¾ cup millet flour

½ cup tapioca flour

2 tablespoons sweet rice flour

2 teaspoons xanthan gum

½ teaspoon sea salt

1½ tablespoons extra-virgin olive oil

## COATING

¼ cup vegan buttery spread, melted

1½ tablespoons nutritional yeast flakes

2 to 5 garlic cloves, minced, or
1½ teaspoons garlic powder

½ teaspoon sea salt

Lightly coat a 12-cup muffin pan with vegan buttery spread.

To make the rolls, put the water in a large measuring cup. Stir in 3 teaspoons of the sugar and the yeast. Let stand for about 5 minutes, until the yeast has bubbled and foamed about ½ inch.

Put the sorghum flour, millet flour, tapioca flour, sweet rice flour, xanthan gum, salt, and remaining 1½ teaspoons of sugar in a heavy-duty stand mixer or a large bowl. Stir with a dry whisk until combined.

Turn the stand mixer or a hand mixer on low speed and gradually add the proofed yeast mixture and oil to make a dough. Turn off the mixer and scrape down the sides of the bowl with a rubber spatula. Resume mixing on medium-high speed for 4 minutes. The dough will be very sticky.

To make the coating, put the vegan buttery spread in a small bowl. Stir in the nutritional yeast, garlic (use the larger amount for a more garlicky taste), and salt until well combined.

With oiled hands, tear off small portions of the dough and roll them between your palms to make small balls, about the size of chestnuts. Dip each ball into the coating. Put four balls in each muffin cup, pressing the balls together slightly. Repeat until all the dough has been used. Let rise uncovered in a warm, draft-free place for about 45 minutes, until doubled in size.

About 10 minutes before the dough is done rising, preheat the oven to 350 degrees F. (If the dough is rising in the oven, be sure to remove it first.)

Bake for 25 to 30 minutes, until golden brown. Let cool in the pan for 2 minutes. Carefully remove the rolls from the pan and put them on a cooling rack. Let cool for 10 minutes. Serve warm.

Per roll: calories: 151, protein: 3 g, fat: 6 g, carbohydrate: 23 g, dietary fiber: 2 g, sodium: 420 mg

This simple-to-prepare flatbread showcases **sweetness** from the chickpea flour, a **spicy** kick from the cumin, and a welcome brightness from the lemon. Enjoy it alongside a thick lentil chili or a silky Indian dahl, or use it to make a sandwich with your favorite fillings.

# CUMIN Flatbread

FREE OF: NIGHTSHADES, NUTS, PEANUTS, SOY

YIELD: 8 TO 10 SERVINGS

1½ cups warm water

1 tablespoon plus 1 teaspoon unrefined cane sugar

2½ teaspoons active dry yeast

2 teaspoons ground flaxseeds

1¼ cups chickpea flour

¾ cup sorghum flour

½ cup tapioca flour

¼ cup arrowroot starch

Grated zest of 1 lemon

2 teaspoons ground cumin

2 teaspoons xanthan gum

1½ teaspoons sea salt, plus more if desired

4 tablespoons extra-virgin olive oil, plus more for handling

½ teaspoon cider vinegar

1 tablespoon sesame seeds

1 tablespoon black sesame seeds

1 tablespoon cumin seeds

Line a baking sheet with aluminum foil.

Put the water in a large measuring cup. Stir in 1 teaspoon of the sugar, the yeast, and flaxseeds. Let stand for about 5 minutes, until the yeast has bubbled and foamed about ½ inch.

Put the chickpea flour, sorghum flour, tapioca flour, arrowroot starch, lemon zest, cumin, xanthan gum, salt, and remaining tablespoon of sugar in a heavy-duty stand mixer or a large bowl. Stir with a dry whisk until combined.

Add 2 tablespoons of the oil and the vinegar to the yeast mixture. Turn the stand mixer or a hand mixer on low speed and gradually add the yeast mixture to the flour mixture to make a dough. Turn off the mixer and scrape down the sides of the bowl with a rubber spatula. Resume mixing on medium-high speed for 5 minutes. The dough will be very sticky, similar to thick muffin batter.

Generously oil the foil on the baking sheet with about 2 tablespoons of the remaining oil. Use the spatula to scrape the dough onto the prepared foil. With oiled hands, spread the dough as thinly as possible without tearing it. Use as much oil as needed. Sprinkle with the sesame seeds and cumin and additional salt if desired. Let rise uncovered in a warm, draft-free place for about 40 minutes, until doubled in size.

About 10 minutes before the dough is done rising, preheat the oven to 425 degrees F. (If the dough is rising in the oven, be sure to remove it first.)

Bake for 40 to 45 minutes, until the edges are golden brown and the top begins to brown. Cut into pieces. Serve warm.

Per serving: calories: 204, protein: 5 g, fat: 8 g, carbohydrate: 26 g, dietary fiber: 4 g, sodium: 365 mg

Baking **pita bread** from scratch may seem like a challenge, but these flatbreads are a **breeze** to prepare. Serve toasted wedges with hummus, or stuff them with your favorite fillings for lunch on the run.

# OVEN-BAKED PITA Pockets

FREE OF: LEGUMES, NIGHTSHADES, NUTS, PEANUTS, SEEDS, SOY          YIELD: 7 TO 8 PITA BREADS

¼ cup warm water, plus 4 to 6 tablespoons

2 teaspoons active dry yeast

1 teaspoon agave nectar

½ cup amaranth flour or quinoa flour

½ cup sorghum flour

½ cup tapioca flour, plus more for rolling

1½ teaspoons xanthan gum

½ teaspoon sea salt

2 tablespoons extra-virgin olive oil

1 teaspoon cider vinegar

Line a baking sheet with parchment paper. Put another baking sheet or a pizza stone in the oven.

Put the ¼ cup of water in a large measuring cup. Stir in the yeast and agave nectar. Let stand for about 5 minutes, until the yeast has bubbled and foamed about ½ inch.

Put the amaranth flour, sorghum flour, tapioca flour, xanthan gum, and salt in a heavy-duty stand mixer or a large bowl. Stir with a dry whisk until combined.

Add the oil and vinegar to the proofed yeast mixture. Using the stand mixer or a hand mixer, beat on low speed and gradually add the yeast mixture to the flour mixture to make a dough. Turn off the mixer and scrape down the sides of the bowl with a rubber spatula. Resume mixing on medium speed. Add the remaining 4 to 6 tablespoons of water, a little at a time, using just enough to create a soft, slightly sticky dough.

Lightly flour a clean work surface. Use a spatula to scrape the dough onto the work surface. Divide the dough into 6 equal portions. Lightly sprinkle each with tapioca flour. Using a lightly floured rolling pin, roll each portion into an oval, about ¼-inch thick, to form the pita breads. Transfer to the lined baking sheet. Repeat with the remaining dough. Let rise uncovered in a warm, draft-free place for 30 to 40 minutes, until doubled in size with puffy areas forming.

About 20 minutes before the dough is done rising, preheat the oven to 500 degrees F. (If the dough is rising in the oven, be sure to remove it first.) The second baking sheet or pizza stone should remain in the oven.

Per pita bread: calories: 128, protein: 3 g, fat: 4 g, carbohydrate: 20 g, dietary fiber: 2 g, sodium: 145 mg

Transfer each piece of dough to the hot baking sheet or pizza stone and bake for 5 to 6 minutes, until the pita breads are puffy and just starting to brown at the edges. Do not over-bake. Carefully remove the pita breads from the baking sheet and put them on a cooling rack. Let cool for 10 minutes.

## TIPS

- Be sure to roll the dough evenly and smoothly. This ensures the pita breads will puff and split like a pocket.

- The short baking time doesn't allow the strong taste of the flours to be cooked out. If you find the taste too strong, feel free to use milder-tasting flours.

This **wholesome** crust can easily stand up to any wheat-based version: it's chewy, crusty, and tender all at the same time. It's not too thick and not too thin, and *just right* for slathering with sauce and topping with lots of fresh vegetables.

# THE Essential PIZZA CRUST

FREE OF: LEGUMES, NIGHTSHADES, PEANUTS, SOY          YIELD: TWO 10-INCH CRUSTS (4 SLICES PER CRUST)

¾ cup plus 3 tablespoons warm water

1 tablespoon ground flaxseeds

2½ teaspoons active dry yeast

2 teaspoons unrefined cane sugar

¾ cup sorghum flour

½ cup tapioca flour

¼ cup arrowroot starch

¼ cup quinoa flour

¼ cup teff flour

2 tablespoons finely ground almonds

1¾ teaspoons xanthan gum

1 teaspoon sea salt

2 tablespoons extra-virgin olive oil, plus more for handling the dough

1 teaspoon cider vinegar

Put a large baking sheet or pizza stone on the bottom rack of the oven. Preheat the oven to 425 degrees F. Let the baking sheet warm for at least 20 minutes, or the pizza stone for at least 45 minutes.

Put the water in a large measuring cup. Stir in the flaxseeds, yeast, and sugar. Let stand for about 5 minutes, until the yeast has bubbled and foamed about ½ inch.

Put the sorghum flour, tapioca flour, arrowroot starch, quinoa flour, teff flour, almonds, xanthan gum, and salt in a heavy-duty stand mixer or a large bowl. Stir with a dry whisk until combined.

Add 2 tablespoons of the oil and the vinegar to the proofed yeast mixture. Turn the stand mixer or a hand mixer on low speed and gradually add the yeast mixture to the flour mixture to make a dough. Turn off the mixer and scrape down the sides of the bowl with a rubber spatula. Resume mixing on medium-high speed for 5 minutes. The dough will be very sticky, similar to thick muffin batter.

Put two sheets of parchment paper on a clean work surface. Lightly coat each sheet with olive oil. Use the spatula to scrape half of the dough onto each sheet.

To form the crusts, use oiled hands to spread both pieces of dough into 8- to 9-inch circles, about ¼-inch thick. Leave a ½- to 1-inch lip around the edges. Prick the top of each with a fork about six times. Let rise uncovered in a warm, draft-free place for about 30 minutes, until the crust is about an inch larger in diameter.

Per slice: calories: 172, protein: 4 g, fat: 5 g, carbohydrate: 28 g, dietary fiber: 3 g, sodium: 269 mg

Put both crusts, along with the parchment paper, on the preheated baking sheet or pizza stone. Bake for 7 to 10 minutes, until the tops of the crusts are slightly firm and the bottoms are crisp. Slide the crusts off the paper onto a cooling rack. Make pizzas or cool and freeze (see tips).

**TIPS**

- To make pizzas, heat the broiler. Brush each crust with 1½ teaspoons of extra-virgin olive oil. Top as desired. Put the pizzas directly on the second oven rack from the top and broil for 8 to 10 minutes, until the toppings are cooked through and the crust is browned. Serve immediately.

- To freeze the pizza crust, let cool, wrap in plastic wrap, and cover with foil. Stored in the freezer, pizza crust will keep for 1 month. Thaw in a preheated oven at 350 degrees F, then top and bake or broil until the toppings have cooked through.

Also called *lathenia*, ladenia is the Greek version of PIZZA. It's similar to the Italian focaccia, a bread dough topped with olive oil, onions, and fresh tomatoes. The name comes from the generous inclusion of OLIVE OIL—ladi means "oil" in Greek. This is one of my favorites.

# Ladenia (OLIVE OIL BREAD)

FREE OF: LEGUMES, NUTS, PEANUTS, SOY                    YIELD: 6 TO 8 SERVINGS

1⅔ cups warm water

2½ teaspoons active dry yeast

1 teaspoon unrefined cane sugar

1½ cups sorghum flour

½ cup arrowroot starch

½ cup quinoa flour

½ cup tapioca flour

2 teaspoons xanthan gum

7 tablespoons extra-virgin olive oil or Greek olive oil, plus more for handling

1 tablespoon ground flaxseeds

1 teaspoon sea salt

½ teaspoon cider vinegar

2 yellow onions, thinly sliced

3 roma tomatoes, cut into ¼-inch slices

2 tablespoons dried oregano

Sea salt

Freshly ground pepper

Line a baking sheet with parchment paper or aluminum foil.

Put the water in a large measuring cup. Stir in the yeast and sugar. Let stand for about 5 minutes, until the yeast has bubbled and foamed about ½ inch.

Put the sorghum flour, arrowroot starch, quinoa flour, tapioca flour, and xanthan gum in a heavy-duty stand mixer or a large bowl. Stir with a dry whisk until combined.

Add 3 tablespoons of the oil, the flaxseeds, salt, and vinegar to the yeast mixture. Turn the stand mixer or a hand mixer on low speed and gradually add the yeast mixture to the flour mixture to make a dough. Turn off the mixer and scrape down the sides of the bowl with a rubber spatula. Resume mixing on medium-high speed for 5 minutes. The dough will be very sticky, similar to thick muffin batter.

Oil the parchment paper on the baking sheet with 2 tablespoons of the remaining oil. Use the spatula to scrape the dough onto the prepared parchment paper. With oiled hands, spread the dough until it is about ¼-inch thick and 1 inch from the sides of the pan. Use as much oil as needed. Let rise uncovered in a warm, draft-free place for about 40 minutes, until doubled in size.

About 10 minutes before the dough is done rising, preheat the oven to 400 degrees F. (If the dough is rising in the oven, be sure to remove it first.)

Use your fingertips to gently indent the top of the dough. Brush with 2 tablespoons of the remaining oil and top with the onions and tomatoes. Sprinkle with the oregano. Season with salt and pepper to taste.

Bake for 40 to 45 minutes, until the edges are golden brown and the onions and tomatoes are cooked through. Cut into pieces. Serve warm.

Per serving: calories: 348, protein: 6 g, fat: 15 g, carbohydrate: 47 g, dietary fiber: 6 g, sodium: 310 mg

Sun-dried tomatoes provide the flavor in this **savory flatbread.** For a sweet version, see Date and Walnut Focaccia (page 95).

# Sun-Dried TOMATO FOCACCIA
# WITH SHALLOTS AND HERBS

FREE OF: LEGUMES, NUTS, PEANUTS, SOY                    YIELD: 8 TO 10 SERVINGS

½ cup sun-dried tomatoes

½ cup plus 2 tablespoons warm water, plus more for soaking the sun-dried tomatoes

1 tablespoon active dry yeast

1 teaspoon unrefined cane sugar

3 tablespoons extra-virgin olive oil, plus more for handling

1 teaspoon pure maple syrup

1 teaspoon cider vinegar

1 cup sorghum flour

½ cup plus 2 tablespoons teff flour

¼ cup arrowroot starch

¼ cup tapioca flour

2 teaspoons xanthan gum

1 teaspoon italian seasoning

¾ teaspoon sea salt

2 shallots, finely chopped

2 tablespoons fresh chopped herbs, such as basil, oregano, rosemary, and thyme

Per serving: calories: 177, protein: 4 g, fat: 5 g, carbohydrate: 29 g, dietary fiber: 4 g, sodium: 244 mg

Line a 9 x 13-inch baking pan with parchment paper. Generously oil the parchment paper.

Put the sun-dried tomatoes in a small bowl. Cover with warm water. Let soak for about 10 minutes, or until soft. Use a fork to transfer the sun-dried tomatoes from the soaking water to a cutting board. Coarsely chop.

Put the ½ cup plus 2 tablespoons of water in a large measuring cup. Stir in the yeast and sugar. Let stand for about 5 minutes, until the yeast has bubbled and foamed about ½ inch.

Pour the soaking water from the sun-dried tomatoes into another large measuring cup. Add enough water to total ½ cup. Stir in 2 tablespoons of the oil, the maple syrup, and vinegar until well combined.

Put the sorghum flour, teff flour, arrowroot starch, tapioca flour, xanthan gum, italian seasoning, and salt in a heavy-duty stand mixer or a large bowl. Stir with a dry whisk until combined.

Turn the stand mixer or a hand mixer on low speed and gradually add the yeast mixture and soaking water to the flour mixture to make a dough. Turn off the mixer and scrape down the sides of the bowl with a rubber spatula. Resume mixing on medium-high speed for 4 minutes. The dough will be very sticky, similar to thick muffin batter.

Use the spatula to scrape the dough into the lined pan. With generously oiled hands, spread the dough in the pan. Do not smooth; the top should remain bumpy (this will give it a rustic appearance). Let rise uncovered in a warm, draft-free place for about 40 minutes, until doubled in size.

About 10 minutes before the dough is done rising, preheat the oven to 400 degrees F. (If the dough is rising in the oven, be sure to remove it first.)

Use your fingers to gently indent the top of the dough. Brush the dough with the remaining tablespoon of oil. Top with the sun-dried tomatoes, shallots, and herbs. Bake for 30 to 40 minutes, until golden brown. Carefully remove the focaccia from the pan and put it on a cooling rack. Let cool for at least 10 minutes before serving. Serve warm.

**TIP:** Instead of topping the focaccia with the sun-dried tomatoes, shallots, and herbs, stir these ingredients directly into the dough after mixing.

## TABLE 12 — Oven temperatures

| FAHRENHEIT (DEGREES F) | CELSIUS (DEGREES C) | GAS MARK |
|---|---|---|
| 175 | 80 | Not available |
| 200 | 95 | ¼ |
| 225 | 110 | ¼ |
| 250 | 120 | ½ |
| 275 | 140 | 1 |
| 300 | 150 | 2 |
| 325 | 160 | 3 |
| 350 | 175 | 4 |
| 375 | 190 | 5 |
| 400 | 205 | 6 |
| 425 | 220 | 7 |
| 450 | 230 | 8 |
| 475 | 240 | 9 |
| 500 | 260 | 10 |

## TABLE 13 — Dry measurements (conventional and metric)

| CONVENTIONAL MEASURE (in ounces) | METRIC MEASURE (exact, in grams) | METRIC MEASURE (standard, in grams) |
|---|---|---|
| 1 | 28.3 | 28 |
| 2 | 56.7 | 57 |
| 3 | 85 | 85 |
| 4 | 113.4 | 125 |
| 5 | 141.7 | 140 |
| 6 | 170.1 | 170 |
| 7 | 198.4 | 200 |
| 8 | 226.8 | 250 |
| 16 | 453.6 | 500 |
| 32 | 907.2 | 1,000 (1 kilogram) |

## PART V

# The Extras

## GLOSSARY

### Equipment

**Baking pans.** Baking pans come in a variety of shapes and sizes, including rectangular, square, and round, as well as those designed for muffins, doughnuts, and novelty shapes. Light-colored metal pans tend to produce a lighter crust, whereas dark metal pans and tend to produce a darker crust and bake more quickly. Nonstick pans are often very dark and produce an uneven result. Glass pans can also be used in place of metal pans. If you are using a dark or glass pan, decrease the oven temperature by 25 degrees. I highly recommend the pans sold at Williams-Sonoma, both in the traditional finish and Goldtouch Nonstick. The Goldtouch pans are made of commercial-grade aluminized steel and are light in color so the oven temperature does not need to be decreased.

**Baking sheets.** Also known as cookie sheets, baking sheets are flat, metal sheets designed for baking and roasting. I often recommend using parchment paper, a silicone baking mat, or a thin layer of oil to line or coat sheets before baking. Similar to baking pans, dark-colored and nonstick baking sheets bake food much more quickly, so use them with care. I get the best results using aluminum baking sheets (which I buy from a local restaurant supply store) lined with parchment paper or a silicone baking mat.

**Cooling racks.** Cooling racks are wire racks set on short legs. This design allows air to circulate around and under freshly baked goods as they cool. Different sizes are available; I prefer large, two-tier racks, which are useful when I bake multiple items.

**Instant-read thermometer.** An instant-read thermometer is a handy kitchen gadget that measures the internal temperature of foods. It is helpful in baking breads leavened with yeast and can be used to ensure that liquids are at the right temperature and that bread is baked through. For more information about testing for doneness, see page 20.

**Loaf pans.** Loaf pans are found in a variety of sizes: 8 x 4-inch, 8½ x 4½-inch, 9 x 5-inch, and 10 x 5-inch are the most common. Darker loaf pans produce a darker, crisper crust, but they can often leave the inside of the bread undercooked. Light-colored loaf pans are ideal for baking quick breads. If you purchase just a single pan, an 8½ x 4½ x 2¾-inch pan (1 pound) is a versatile option. I highly recommend Williams-Sonoma 1-pound Goldtouch Nonstick pan, which improved the rise on all of my breads.

**Parchment paper.** Parchment paper is used to line baking sheets to create a nonstick surface. It is disposable. Silicone baking mats are good, reusable alternatives (Silpat is a popular brand).

**Pastry bags.** Pastry bags, or piping bags, are cone- or triangular-shaped bags made from cloth, paper, or plastic. When the bag is squeezed, the contents are forced through the tip. Pastry bags are handy for decorating cakes and cupcakes and for piping breadsticks. Make a homemade pastry bag by snipping a bottom corner off a large ziplock bag.

**Pastry blender.** A pastry blender is used to cut cold fat into dry ingredients when making biscuits, crusts, and scones. This tool also is helpful for mashing soft ingredients, such as avocados and bananas.

**Rolling pin.** A rolling pin is a cylindrical kitchen tool used to flatten dough. There are two styles: roller-style pins have a thick roller with small handles on the ends, and rod, or french rolling pins, are thinner with tapered ends. Both kinds are usually made from wood, but glass, marble, silicone, and stainless steel rolling pins exist. I prefer to use a french-style wooden rolling pin.

**Spatula, silicone or rubber.** A spatula is used for scraping mixing bowls, smoothing batter or dough, and folding ingredients together. Silicone or rubber spatulas are flexible, heat resistant, sturdy, and have smooth edges.

Also see Kitchen Equipment (page 23) for more recommendations.

## Ingredients and Food Terms

**Agave nectar.** Made from the agave plant, agave nectar is a liquid sweetener that can be used in place of honey, pure maple syrup, sugar, and other sweeteners. Agave nectar is naturally sweeter than sugar, and its low glycemic index may make it tolerable for diabetics.

**Almond butter.** Almond butter is a nut paste made from almonds. It is a slightly sweet and popular alternative to peanut butter. Almonds are high in good-for-you monounsaturated fats and an excellent source of calcium, fiber, magnesium, and vitamin E.

**Baking powder.** Baking powder is a chemical leavening agent that helps batters rise. In vegan baking, it also assists in binding ingredients. When a recipe calls for both baking powder and baking soda, the baking powder does the majority of the leavening, while the baking soda adds tenderness. Too much baking powder can cause a bitter taste or make baked goods collapse; too little will create a tough product that does not rise properly. Baking powder contains cornstarch. If you are allergic or sensitive to corn, see page 22 for substitutions.

**Baking soda.** Also known as sodium bicarbonate, baking soda is a chemical leavener that is about four times stronger than baking powder. It is used in recipes that contain an acid, such as citrus juice, molasses, vegan buttermilk, or vinegar. Baking soda begins to react right away, so be sure to bake the batter quickly after mixing. Too much baking soda will result in a coarse, dry crumb or soapy taste.

**Biscotti.** Biscotti means "twice-baked" and refers to a long, often dry and hard cookie designed for dunking in coffee or tea. The dough is baked in a log form, then cooled, sliced, and returned to the oven to bake on low heat until crisp.

**Brown rice syrup.** Brown rice syrup is a sweetener derived from malted brown rice. It can be used in place of agave nectar or pure maple syrup.

**Butter.** Butter is a dairy product that is produced by churning cream and separating the fat from the liquid. It is not vegan. Vegan buttery spread is an excellent substitute for butter. The brand I most recommend is Earth Balance (available both in soy-based and soy-free versions). For more information about vegan butter replacements, see page 17.

**Buttermilk.** Buttermilk is a dairy-based beverage that is creamy, tangy, and thick. For information about vegan buttermilk replacements, see page 17.

**Carob powder.** Made from the ground seed pods of the leguminous carob tree, carob powder is dark brown and rich tasting. It is caffeine-free and naturally sweet and is often used as a substitute for cocoa powder.

**Cocoa powder.** Cocoa powder is produced from pressed chocolate liquor. The cocoa butter is removed, then processed to make a fine powder. There are two types of unsweetened cocoa powder: natural and dutch-process. Natural cocoa powder is very bitter and has a deep chocolate flavor. It reacts with baking soda to create leavening action. Dutch-process cocoa powder is treated with an alkali to neutralize cocoa's natural acidity. It is milder than natural cocoa powder and has a rich but delicate flavor.

**Coconut, shredded dried.** Shredded dried coconut is designed for baking and is typically sweetened. The recipes in this book are formulated with unsweetened shredded dried coconut, which is available at most natural foods stores. Edward and Sons is a favorite brand.

**Coconut milk.** Coconut milk is a sweet, white liquid derived from the meat of a coconut. It is not a dairy product.

**Coconut oil.** Coconut oil is extracted from the meat of a coconut. It can be substituted for vegan buttery spread or other oils. For more information about coconut oil, see page 18.

**Confectioners' sugar.** Also known as powdered sugar or icing sugar, confectioners' sugar is granulated sugar that has been ground to a powder and combined with cornstarch to prevent clumping or crystallization. Be sure to check product labels; some brands are ground with wheat starch.

**Dough.** Dough is an unbaked mass of ingredients that can be kneaded or rolled. It has a thicker consistency—and generally less fat, liquid, and sugar—than batter.

**Egg replacer.** Commercial powdered egg replacer is made from carbohydrate gum, leavening (calcium carbonate, calcium lactate, and citric acid), potato starch, and tapioca flour. For each egg, use 1½ teaspoons of egg replacer whisked with 2 tablespoons of water, unless the recipe indicates otherwise. For other egg replacements, see page 18.

**Flaxseeds.** Flaxseeds are brown or golden seeds that contain soluble fiber, cancer-fighting lignans, and omega-3 fatty acids. In most instances, they should be ground before using; grind flaxseeds in a coffee grinder or purchase them in ground form (labeled "flax meal" or "flaxseed meal"). Store flaxseeds in the refrigerator or freezer.

**Hempseeds.** Hempseeds are highly nutritious seeds from the *Cannabis sativa* plant; however, they do not contain psychoactive properties. There are an excellent source of protein and have the optimal balance of omega-3 to omega-6 fatty acids.

**Maple syrup, pure.** Pure maple syrup has a rich, sweet flavor. It is produced from the sap of maple trees and comes in different grades. In general, there are two broad classifications of maple syrup: grade A (also called "grade 1," "extra light," or "light") and grade B (also called "grade 2," "amber," or "dark amber"). Either kind may be used in recipes or for passing at the table. Pure maple syrup should not be confused with pancake syrup, which is a sugary processed food.

**Milk.** For more information about milk replacements, see page 16.

**Molasses.** Molasses is a thick syrup that is separated from raw cane sugar during the sugar-making process. There are different varieties of molasses. Light molasses comes from the first boiling of the sugar syrup and is light in flavor and color. Dark molasses comes from the second boiling and has a deeper color and flavor. Blackstrap molasses comes from the third boiling and is rich in iron and has an intense flavor.

**Nondairy milk.** For more information about milk replacements, see page 16.

**Nut or seed butter.** Nut butters are made from ground nuts. Popular varieties include almond, cashew, and peanut butters. Seed butters, such as tahini, are made from ground seeds. I recommend using natural, roasted varieties for the most flavor, with the only ingredient being the nut or seed itself. When opening a new jar of nut or seed butter, mix in the natural oil that separates out and rises to the top. If you pour off the oil, the nut or seed butter will be rock hard instead of creamy and spreadable. Store nut and seed butters in the refrigerator after opening to prevent the oil from separating out and extend the butter's shelf life.

**Nutritional yeast flakes.** Nutritional yeast is an inactive form of yeast that is high in B vitamins and has a pleasant cheesy taste. It is sold as flakes.

**Peanut butter.** Peanut butter is made from roasted peanuts that are ground to a paste. See nut butter above.

**Quinoa.** Pronounced KEEN-wah, quinoa is a high-protein seed with a mild, nutty taste. Typically used like a grain, quinoa also is ground into a versatile gluten-free flour. For information about quinoa flour, see page 13.

**Rind.** See zest (page 127).

**Streusel.** A crumbly mixture made of fat, flour, sugar, and often spices, streusel is used as a sweet, textured topping for baked goods, such as coffee cakes, muffins, and pies. The term is derived from the German word *streuen*, which means to sprinkle or scatter.

**Sugar.** In baking, sugar not only sweetens but also adds color, tenderness, texture, and volume to baked goods and acts as a preservative. Sugar comes in many forms. For information about the sugar varieties used in this book, see agave nectar (page 123), confectioners' sugar (page 124), maple syrup (page 125), molasses (page 125), and unrefined cane sugar (below).

**Tahini.** Tahini is a paste made from ground sesame seeds. It is typically used in Middle Eastern and Mediterranean cuisines and is somewhat bitter. Available either raw or roasted, tahini is a key ingredient in hummus but also adds a pleasant flavor to baked goods.

**Unrefined cane sugar.** As its name indicates, unrefined cane sugar is minimally processed, which leaves minerals, trace elements, and vitamins intact. Unrefined cane sugar imparts the same sweetness as refined sugar, with a hint of molasses flavor that adds depth to baked goods. I prefer Sucanat, the brand made by Wholesome Sweeteners.

**Vanilla.** Vanilla, a popular flavoring, is sold as a bean in its whole form; in baking, vanilla extract is typically used. To make your own vanilla extract, cut a whole vanilla bean in half lengthwise and put it in ¾ cup of vodka. Seal and let steep for at least 6 months.

**Yeast.** Baker's yeast is used to leaven baked goods. While baking powder and soda react chemically, yeast is a living organism that produces a rise by feeding on the dough. Yeast can be fresh (also known as compressed cakes) or dry (dehydrated granules). Fresh yeast is ivory in color, moist, soft, and very perishable. Dry yeast has been pressed and dried; it becomes active when mixed with a warm liquid. There are two kinds of dry yeast: regular active dry yeast and instant, or rapid-rise, yeast. For more information, see Yeast Breads (page 71).

**Zest.** The zest is the colorful outer rind of citrus fruit. Rich in flavor, zest can be removed using a grater, knife, vegetable peeler, or zester. The white pith inside the zest is very bitter and should be avoided.

## Techniques

**Beat.** To beat a mixture is to use a spoon, wire whisk, or an electric mixer to stir with a brisk movement until the mixture is smooth. When using a stand mixer, use the paddle attachment.

**Blend.** To blend is to process two or more ingredients in a food processor or blender until smooth and uniform.

**Boil.** To boil is to heat water or other liquids in a saucepan on high heat until bubbles form, rising steadily and breaking the surface.

**Cut in.** To cut solid fats into dry ingredients when making dough for biscuits, pastries, or scones, use two knives, a pastry blender, your fingertips, or a food processor. Continue until the mixture resembles coarse crumbs.

**Drizzle.** To drizzle means to pour a thin stream of liquid, such as a glaze or melted chocolate, over baked goods, such as breads, coffee cakes, and cookies.

**Dust.** To dust a food, pan, or work surface is to coat it lightly with cocoa powder, confectioners' sugar, or flour. For example, cocoa powder can be used to coat pans before chocolate cake batter is added. Confectioners' sugar is often dusted over finished desserts or sweet breads for aesthetic reasons and to impart a little extra sweetness. Flour is often used on work surfaces for rolling dough or inside an oiled pan to prevent sticking.

**Grate.** To grate a food item, use a wide box grater or the grating attachment of a food processor. Grated fruits and vegetables are sometimes used in baked goods, such as zucchini bread. Be sure to drain and squeeze grated fruits and vegetables well to remove excess moisture before using, unless the recipe indicates otherwise.

**Knead.** To knead dough, work it with the heels of your hands, using a pressing and folding motion. Gluten-containing yeast dough requires a significant amount of kneading. In comparison, gluten-free yeast dough requires minimal kneading. For example, when making biscuits, pastries, and scones, knead the dough only a few times, just until it comes together.

**Mix.** To mix is to stir two or more ingredients until they are evenly combined. Mixing can be done in a blender or food processor, with a mixer, or manually with a spoon and bowl.

**Proof.** Proofing is a technique used to determine whether active dry yeast is alive. This is achieved by dissolving the yeast in a warm liquid with flour or sugar, then letting the mixture stand for about 5 minutes, until the yeast has bubbled and foamed about ½ inch. Yeast is temperature sensitive, so using a thermometer is helpful. If the liquid is

- 50 degrees F (10 degrees C) or cooler, the yeast will be inactive;
- 60 to 70 degrees F (15 to 21 degrees C), the yeast action will be slow;
- 90 to 100 degrees F (32 to 38 degrees C), the yeast is at an ideal temperature;
- 104 to 134 degrees F (40 to 57 degrees C), the yeast action will be slow;
- 138 degrees F (58 degrees C) or warmer, the yeast will die.

**Scrape down.** To scrape down dough is to move a firm rubber or silicone spatula around the inside of a bowl, reincorporating any loose bits into the dough mixture. This method ensures all ingredients will be mixed thoroughly.

**Score.** To score is to create shallow cuts in dough with a sharp knife.

**Sift.** To sift is to use a sieve to break up clumps and aerate dry ingredients. Recipes can indicate whether to sift the ingredient before or after measuring. For the recipes in this book, measures are given for dry ingredients *before* they are sifted.

**Whisk.** To whisk is to rapidly beat air into a moist mixture by using a wire whisk or electric mixer. Dry ingredients are often stirred with a whisk to combine them.

## Other

**Dash.** A dash is a measurement equivalent to ¹⁄₁₆ teaspoon.

**Pinch.** A pinch is an inexact measurement that refers to using the thumb and forefinger to pick up a small amount of a dry ingredient. A pinch is equivalent to about ¹⁄₁₆ teaspoon.

**Scant.** If a recipe calls for a "scant" teaspoon, tablespoon, cup, or other measurement, just barely fill the measuring spoon or cup.

## SUPPLIERS AND RESOURCES

H ere is a listing of retailers that sell gluten-free vegan products. Because manufacturers change their formulations, be sure to always read labels, even on products that you've used many times before. In addition, try to keep tabs on companies and their manufacturing procedures to make sure they remain gluten-free.

### Bob's Red Mill

bobsredmill.com

Bob's Red Mill manufactures both gluten-free and gluten-containing baking aids, beans, flaxseeds, flour, and grains. Specially marked packages indicate products that were produced in dedicated gluten-free, casein-free facilities.

### Free From Market

freefrommarket.com

Free From Market carries common and hard-to-find allergen-free products, including gluten-free, low-carbohydrate, low-protein, and vegan groceries, along with body and skin care, cleaners, supplements, and more. The company does not carry products with "may contain" labels or those that contain artificial sweeteners, dyes, or genetically modified organisms.

### GlutenFree.com

glutenfree.com

GlutenFree.com has been catering to people with celiac disease and those with restricted diets since 1993. The website features a wide variety of baked goods, baking supplies, books, mixes, snacks, vitamins, and more.

### The Gluten-Free Mall

glutenfreemall.com

The Gluten-Free Mall has offered online shopping since 1998 and carries a wide selection of casein-free, gluten-free, wheat-free, and other allergen-free foods and dietary products.

### King Arthur Flour

kingarthurflour.com

America's oldest flour company, King Arthur Flour began manufacturing flour in 1790. The company recently added a gluten-free multipurpose mix—which is also allergen-free and certified kosher—that is packed at a dedicated gluten-free facility.

### Kinnikinnick Foods

kinnikinnick.com

Kinnikinnick Foods is dedicated to providing risk-free foods for people with celiac disease and those with autism and other dietary requirements. Products include gluten-free bagels, breads, and doughnuts, and many flours, leaveners, and other baking supplies, most of which are also dairy- and soy-free.

### Pangea Vegan Products

veganstore.com

Pangea is an online store that offers a comprehensive selection of high-quality, cruelty-free, nonanimal-derived products, including body care, books, food, clothing, DVDs, pet products, and more.

### VeganEssentials

veganessentials.com

VeganEssentials is one of American's oldest cruelty-free online retailers. Vegan owned and operated, the company specializes in high-quality animal-free products, including gluten-free items.

### Viva Vegan Store

vivagranolaveganstore.ca

Viva Vegan Store is a Canadian online store that is owned and operated by vegans. Products include books, clothing, cosmetics, crafts, DVDs, food, skin and body care, and supplements. Gluten-free and kosher items are available.

## RESOURCES

### Celiac Disease and Gluten-Free

Canadian Celiac Association (celiac.ca)

Celiac.com

Celiac Disease Foundation (celiac.org)

Celiac Sprue Association (csaceliacs.org)

Glutenfreedom.net (including Raising Our Celiac Kids (ROCK))

Gluten-Free Living Magazine (glutenfreeliving.com)

Gluten Intolerance Group (gluten.net)

### Food Allergies

Allergic Living Magazine (allergicliving.com)

Living Without Magazine (livingwithout.com)

Food Allergy and Anaphylaxis Network (foodallergy.org)

Food Allergy Initiative (faiusa.org)

*For additional resources, updates, and information, please see my website: lauriesadowski.com*

# Index

Table references are indicated by a *t*.

## A

agave nectar, 123
allergens, 2–3
Almond Breakfast Biscuits, Sticky, 48
almond butter
    about, 123
    and Buckwheat Muffins, 41
almond flour, 15
Amaranth Crackers, Crunchy, 59
amaranth flour, 10, 15
Animal Crackers, Cheezy, 58
Apple Cider and Buckwheat Bread, 77
apples
    -Chai Scones, 44
    in Cornbread and Wild Rice Stuffing with Pecans, 69
    -Cornmeal Muffins, 37
    Spice Cake with Vanilla Glaze, 96–97
arrowroot starch, 10–11, 15
autoimmune disorders, 1

## B

Babka, Grandma's Polish, 78–79
Bagels, New York-Style, 106–107
baking
    gluten-free, about, 2
    troubleshooting, 27
baking pans, 23, 24*t*, 121
baking powder
    about, 123
    substitutions for, 22
baking sheets, 121

baking soda
    about, 123
    substitutions for, 22
bananas
    in Buckwheat and Almond Butter Muffins, 41
    -Chocolate Chip Bread, 29
    -Nut Monkey Bread, 82
    -Rhubarb Crumble Muffins, 42
Bannock, Chickpea, 68
barley, 4
Basil and Corn Spoon Bread, 56
Beer Bread, Hearty, 52
biscotti
    about, 123
    Peppercorn-Rye, 61
biscuits
    Almond, Sticky, 48
    "Buttermilk," Basic, 63
    Cheezy Dinner, Easy, 65
    Maple-Pumpkin, Gooey, 47
    Olive Oil with Roasted Garlic, Rosemary, and Hempseeds, 64
    Sweet Potato and Buckwheat, 62
Blackberry-Cornmeal Muffins, 37
blender, pastry, 122
blueberries
    -Cornmeal Muffins, 37
    Scones, 45
breads. *See* quick breads; yeast breads
breadsticks
    Italian, 104
    Peppercorn-Rye Biscotti, 61
    Pumpernickel, Soft, 103
    Raisin-Orange with Vanilla Glaze, 90–91

brown rice syrup, 123
bubble bread, Banana-Nut Monkey, 82
buckwheat
    and Almond Butter Muffins, 41
    and Apple Cider Bread, 77
    flour, about, 11, 15
    Pancakes, Overnight, 83
    and Sweet Potato Biscuits, 62
    Tortillas, 67
buns. *See also* rolls
    Breakfast, with Cranberries and Pecans, 84–85
    Burger, 108–109
    Cinnamon, Breakfast, 88–89
butter
    about, 123
    nut or seed, 125
    substitutions for, 17–18
buttermilk, vegan
    about, 17, 123
    Biscuits, Basic, 63
buttery spread, vegan, 17

## C

Cake, Apple Spice with Vanilla Glaze, 96–97
calories, decreasing, 16
canola oil, 18
cardamom
    -Pear (-Peach) Bread, 30
carob powder, 124
celiac disease, 1, vi–vii
Chai-Apple Scones, 44
Cheezy Animal Crackers, 58
Cheezy Dinner Biscuits, Easy, 65
chestnut flour, 11, 15

chickpea flour, 11, 15
chocolate
    Cocoa-Pumpkin Loaf, 31
    Double-Chocolate Hazelnut
        Bread, 80
    Double-Chocolate Muffins, 39
    -Filled Pumpkin Cinnamon Rolls
        with Orange Glaze, 86–87
    in Mexican Mole Bread, 100
chocolate chips
    -Banana Bread, 29
    in Buckwheat Pancakes, Over-
        night, 83
    in Double-Chocolate Hazelnut
        Bread, 80
    in Peanut Butter Muffins, 40
    Scones, 46
Cider, Buckwheat Bread and, 77
cinnamon
    Buns, Breakfast, 88–89
    in Maple-Raisin Bread, 76
    Rolls, Chocolate-Filled Pumpkin,
        with Orange Glaze, 86–87
    -Sugar Doughnuts, 93
    -Sweet Potato Bread, 32
cocoa powder
    about, 124
    Chocolate-Filled Pumpkin Cinna-
        mon Rolls with Orange Glaze,
        86–87
    Double-Chocolate Hazelnut
        Bread, 80
    Double-Chocolate Muffins, 39
    in Mexican Mole Bread, 100
    -Pumpkin Loaf, 31
    substitutions for, 22
coconut
    flour, 11, 15
    milk, 16–17, 124
    oil, 18, 124
    Pull-Apart Bread, 81
    shredded dried, 124
confectioner's sugar
    about, 124
    substitutions for, 22
cooking techniques, 14–16, 127–128
cooling racks, 23, 122
cornbread
    Corn and Basil Spoon Bread, 56

Maple-Kissed, 55
and Wild Rice Stuffing with
    Apples and Pecans, 69
corn flour, 11, 15
cornmeal
    about, 11–12
    -Blackberry Muffins, 37
cornstarch, 12, 15
crackers
    Amaranth, Crunchy, 59
    Animal, Cheezy, 58
    Polenta, In-a-Pinch, 57
cranberries
    in Breakfast Buns with Pecans,
        84–85
    in Fruit and Nut Crisps, 60
    -Maple Biscuits, Gooey, 47
    Upside-Down Muffins, 38
Crisps, Fruit and Nut, 60
Crohn's disease, 6
cross-contamination with gluten,
    4–6
Cumin Flatbread, 113

D
dairy products, 4
Date and Walnut Focaccia, 95
Deep-Fried Glazed Doughnuts,
    92–93
Dijon and Thyme, in Rolls, Crusty,
    110
Dinner Rolls, Sweet, 111
doneness, testing for, 20
dough, about, 124
doughnuts
    Cinnamon-Sugar, 92–93
    Deep-Fried Glazed, 92–93
    Maple-Glazed Baked, 49

E
Easy Cheezy Dinner Biscuits, 65
eggs
    about, 4
    substitutions for, 18, 19t, 124
English Muffins, Easy, 105
equipment, 23t, 73, 121–122

F
fat, decreasing, 14–16

fava bean flour, 15
fillings
    apple, 96
    for Chocolate-Filled Pumpkin
        Cinnamon Rolls with Orange
        Glaze, 87
    for Cinnamon Buns, Breakfast, 89
flatbreads
    Cumin, 113
    Date and Walnut, 95
    Ladenia (Olive Oil Bread), 118
    Pita Pockets, Oven-Baked, 114
    Pizza Crust, The Essential,
        116–117
    Sun-Dried Tomato Focaccia with
        Shallots and Herbs, 119
Flax Bread, Wholesome, 99
flaxseeds, 124–125
flour
    gluten-free, 10–14
    substitutions for, 22
focaccia. See also flatbreads
    Date and Walnut, 95
    Ladenia (Olive Oil Bread), 118
    Sun-Dried Tomato with Shallots
        and Herbs, 119
food labels, 3–4
food substitutions, 7, 16–19, 22,
    124
food terms and ingredients, 123–127
freezing baked goods, 20
French Bread, Rustic, 102
Fritters, Peach with Lemon Glaze,
    Baked, 94
Fruit and Nut Crisps, 60
Fry Bread, Chickpea, 68

G
garfava flour, 12, 15
Garlicky Pull-Apart Rolls, 112
Gingerbread, Old-Fashioned, 34
glazes
    for doughnuts, 93
    Lemon, 94
    Orange, 87
    Vanilla, 91
gluten
    about, 1
    cross-contamination of, 4–6

gluten-free
  baking, 2
  flours and starches, 10–14
  oats, 12
  pantry staples, 21t
Grandma's Polish Babka, 78–79
guar gum, 9–10

**H**
Hazelnut Bread, Double-Chocolate, 80
hazelnut flour, 15
hempseeds
  about, 125
  Bread, Multigrain, 101
  in Olive Oil Biscuits with Roasted Garlic and Rosemary, 64
Herbed Biscuits, 63

**I**
ingredients
  pantry staples, 21t
  substitutions for, 7, 16–19, 22, 124
  temperature of, 18
  terms for, 4, 123–127
Italian Breadsticks, 104

**J**
Jam and PB Muffins, 40

**K**
kitchen equipment, 23t, 121–122

**L**
labels, food, 3–4
Ladenia (Olive Oil Bread), 118
legumes, as allergens, 2
loaf pans, 122

**M**
maple syrup
  in Breakfast Buns with Cranberries and Pecans, 84–85
  Cornbread, 55
  -Glazed Doughnuts, Baked, 49
  -Pumpkin Biscuits, Gooey, 47
  -Raisin Bread, 76
  substitutions for, 22

maple syrup, pure, 125
masa harina, 11
measurements, dry, 120t
measuring spoons and cups, 24t
meat, substitutions for, 7
methods, cooking, 127–128
Mexican Mole Bread, 100
milk, substitutions for, 16–17
millet flour
  about, 12, 15
  -Molasses Bread, 54
molasses
  about, 125
  -Millet Bread, 54
Mole Bread, Mexican 100
Monkey Bread, Banana-Nut, 82
muffins
  Back-of-the-Box Raisin, 36
  Banana-Rhubarb Crumble, 42
  Blackberry-Cornmeal, 37
  Buckwheat and Almond Butter, 41
  Cranberry Upside-Down, 38
  Double-Chocolate, 39
  English, Easy, 105
  PB and J, 40
  Sugarcoated Muffin Bites, 35
Multigrain Hempseed Bread, 101

**N**
New York-Style Bagels, 106–107
nightshades, 2
nutritional content and weight of gluten-free flours, 15t
nutritional yeast flakes, 125
nuts
  as allergens, 2–3
  butter from, 125
  flours from, 12
  milk from, 17
  toasting, 20

**O**
oats, 12
obesity, 6
olive oil
  about, 18
  Biscuits with Roasted Garlic, Rosemary, and Hempseeds, 64

Bread (Ladenia), 118
Olives and Sun-Dried Tomato Zucchini Bread, Mediterranean, 53
Orange Glaze, 87
Orange-Raisin Breadsticks with Vanilla Glaze, 90–91

**P**
Pancakes, Buckwheat, Overnight, 83
pans
  baking, 23, 24t, 121
  loaf, 122
parchment paper, 19, 23, 122
pastry bags, 122
pastry blender, 122
PB and J Muffins, 40
peaches
  -Cardamom Bread, 30
  -Cornmeal Muffins, 37
  Fritters with Lemon Glaze, Baked, 94
peanut butter, 125
  in Double-Chocolate Bread, 80
  PB and J Muffins, 40
peanuts, as allergens, 3
Pear-Cardamom Bread, 30
pecans
  in Breakfast Buns with Cranberries, 84–85
  in Cornbread and Wild Rice Stuffing with Apples, 69
  in Fruit and Nut Crisps, 60
  in Maple-Pumpkin Biscuits, Gooey, 47
Peppercorn-Rye Biscotti, 61
Pita Pockets, Oven-Baked, 114–115
pizza
  Crust, The Essential, 116–117
  Ladenia (Olive Oil Bread), 118
polenta
  Corn and Basil Spoon Bread, 56
  Crackers, In-a-Pinch, 57
potatoes
  flour from, 12, 15
  milk from, 17
  starch from, 12–13, 15
potatoes, sweet
  and Buckwheat Biscuits, 62

Cinnamon-Swirled Sweet Potato
Bread, 32
Pumpernickel Breadsticks, Soft, 103
pumpkin
-Cocoa Loaf, 31
-Maple Biscuits, Gooey, 47

**Q**
quick breads
about, 25–27
savory
Amaranth Crackers, Crunchy,
59
Animal Crackers, Cheezy, 58
Beer Bread, Hearty, 52
Buckwheat Tortillas, 67
"Buttermilk" Biscuits, Basic,
63
Chickpea Bannock (Fry Bread),
68
Corn and Basil Spoon Bread,
56
Cornbread, Maple-Kissed, 55
Cornbread and Wild Rice
Stuffing with Apples and
Pecans, 69
Dinner Biscuits, Cheezy, 65
Fruit and Nut Crisps, 60
Millet-Molasses Bread, 54
Olive Oil Biscuits with Roasted
Garlic, Rosemary, and
Hempseeds, 64
Peppercorn-Rye Biscotti, 61
Polenta Crackers, In-a-Pinch,
57
Scones, Spicy Southwest, 66
Soda Bread, Simple, 51
Sweet Potato and Buckwheat
Biscuits, 62
Zucchini, Mediterranean, 53
sweet
Almond Breakfast Biscuits,
Sticky, 48
Apple-Chai Scones, 44
Banana-Rhubarb Crumble
Muffins, 42
Blackberry-Cornmeal Muffins,
37
Blueberry Scones, Wild, 45
Buckwheat and Almond Butter

Muffins, 41
Chocolate Chip-Banana Bread,
29
Chocolate Chip Scones, 46
Cinnamon-Swirled Sweet
Potato Bread, 32
Cocoa-Pumpkin Loaf, 31
Cranberry Upside-Down Muf-
fins, 38
Double-Chocolate Muffins, 39
Gingerbread, Old-Fashioned,
34
Maple-Glazed Doughnuts,
Baked, 49
Maple-Pumpkin Biscuits,
Gooey, 47
PB and J Muffins, 40
Pear- (Peach-) Cardamom
Bread, 30
Quinoa-Raisin Breakfast Bread,
33
Raisin Muffins, Back-of-the-
Box, 36
Raspberry-Tahini Scones, 43
Sugarcoated Muffin Bites, 35
quinoa
about, 126
flour, 13, 15
how to cook, 33
-Raisin Breakfast Bread, 33

**R**
racks, cooling, 122
raisins
Back-of-the-Box Muffins, 36
-Maple Biscuits, Gooey, 47
-Maple Bread, 76
-Orange Breadsticks with Vanilla
Glaze, 90–91
-Quinoa Breakfast Bread, 33
substitutions for, 22
Raspberry-Tahini Scones, 43
Rhubarb-Banana Crumble Muffins,
42
rice
and Cornbread Stuffing with
Apples and Pecans, 69
flour, 13, 15
milk, 17
rind (zest), 127

rolling pins, 23, 122
rolls. *See also* buns
Chocolate-Filled Pumpkin Cinnamon with Orange Glaze, 86–87
with Dijon and Thyme, Crusty,
110
Dinner, Sweet, 111
Garlicky Pull-Apart, 112
Rye-Peppercorn Biscotti, 61

**S**
scones
Apple-Chai, 44
Blueberry, Wild, 45
Chocolate Chip, 46
Raspberry-Tahini, 43
Spicy Southwest, 66
seeds
as allergens, 3
butter from, 125
milk from, 17
toasting, 20
soda, baking
about, 123
Soda Bread, Simple, 51
sorghum flour, 13, 15
soy
as allergen, 3
flour, 13, 15
milk, 17
spatulas, 23, 122
Spice Cake, Apple, with Vanilla
Glaze, 96–97
Spicy Southwest Scones, 66
starches, gluten-free, 10–14
storage of baked goods, 20
streusel, 126
Stuffing, Cornbread and Wild Rice
with Apples and Pecans, 69
Submarine Sandwich Buns, 108–109
substitutes, food, 7, 16–19, 22, 124
sugar
about, 126
confectioner's, 22, 124
decreasing, 16
substitutions for, 22
unrefined, cane, 126
Sugarcoated Muffin Bites, 35
suppliers, 129–130
sweeteners, decreasing, 16

sweet potatoes
    and Buckwheat Biscuits, 62
    Cinnamon-Swirled Sweet Potato
      Bread, 32

**T**
tahini
    about, 126
    -Raspberry Scones, 43
tapioca flour, 13, 15
techniques
    customizing recipes, 14–16
    general baking, 18–20, 127–128
    for glazing, 26
    for perfect biscuits and scones,
      27
    for perfect loaves and muffins, 26
    testing for doneness, 73
teff flour, 14, 15
temperature
    of ingredients, 18
    oven, 120*t*
thermometer, instant-read, 73, 122
Thyme and Dijon, in Rolls, Crusty,
    110
tomatoes, sun-dried
    Focaccia with Shallots and Herbs,
      119
    in Zucchini Bread, Mediterra-
      nean, 53
Tortillas, Buckwheat, 67
troubleshooting baking problems, 27

**V**
vanilla
    about, 126
    Glaze, 91, 96
veganism, about, 6–7
vinegar, substitutions for, 22

**W**
walnuts
    and Date Focaccia, 95
    in Maple-Pumpkin Biscuits,
      Gooey, 47
wheat products, 4. *See also* gluten;
    gluten-free
Wild Blueberry Scones, 45

**X**
xantham gum, 9–10

**Y**
yeast
    about, 72, 126
    substitutions for, 22
yeast breads
    about, 71–74
    savory
      Bagels, New York-Style,
        106–107
      Buns, Burger, 108–109
      Cumin Flatbread, 113
      Dijon and Thyme Rolls,
        Crusty, 110
      Dinner Rolls, Sweet, 111
      English Muffins, Easy, 105
      Flax Bread, Wholesome, 99
      French Bread, Rustic, 102
      Garlicky Pull-Apart Rolls, 112
      Hempseed Bread, Multigrain,
        101
      Italian Breadsticks, 104
      Ladenia (Olive Oil Bread), 118
      Mexican Mole Bread, 100
      Pita Pockets, Oven-Baked,
        114–115
      Pizza Crust, The Essential,
        116–117
      Pumpernickel Breadsticks, Soft,
        103
      Sun-Dried Tomato Focaccia
        with Shallots and Herbs,
        119
    sweet
      Apple Cider and Buckwheat
        Bread, 77
      Apple Spice Cake with Vanilla
        Glaze, 96–97
      Babka, Grandma's Polish,
        78–79
      Banana-Nut Monkey Bread,
        82
      Chocolate-Filled Pumpkin Cin-
        namon Rolls with Orange
        Glaze, 86–87
      Cinnamon Buns, Breakfast,
        88–89
      Coconut Pull-Apart Bread, 81
      Cranberries and Pecans in
        Breakfast Buns, 84–85
      Date and Walnut Focaccia,
        95
      Double-Chocolate Hazelnut
        Bread, 80
      Doughnuts, Deep-Fried Glazed,
        92–93
      Maple-Raisin Bread, 76
      Pancakes, Overnight, 83
      Peach Fritters with Lemon
        Glaze, Baked, 94
      Raisin-Orange Breadsticks with
        Vanilla Glaze, 90–91
yeast flakes, nutritional, 125

**Z**
zest, 127
Zucchini Bread, Mediterranean, 53

# Book Publishing Co.

Community owned since 1974

*books that educate, inspire, and empower*

To find your favorite vegetarian products online, visit:

**www.healthy-eating.com**

### Food Allergy Survival Guide
*Vesanto Melina, RD,*
*Jo Stepaniak, MSEd,*
*Dina Aronson, RD*
978-1-57067-163-0    $19.95

### Food Allergies
*Vesanto Melina, RD,*
*Jo Stepaniak, MSEd,*
*Dina Aronson, RD*
978-1-55312-046-9    $11.95

### Allergen-Free Baking
*Jill Robbins*
978-0-9776836-1-1    $18.95

### Eat Vegan on $4 a Day
*Ellen Jaffe Jones*
978-1-57067-257-6    $14.95

### Local Bounty
*Devra Gartenstein*
978-1-57067-219-4    $17.95

### Simple Treats
*Ellen Abraham*
978-1-57067-137-1    $14.95

Purchase these health titles and cookbooks from your local bookstore or natural food store,
or you can buy them directly from:

Book Publishing Company  •  P.O. Box 99  •  Summertown, TN 38483  •  1-800-695-2241

*Please include $3.95 per book for shipping and handling.*